KEN WHITEHEAD'S

COARSE FISHING SKILLS

Illustrated by Russell Birkett

BLANDFORD

A BLANDFORD BOOK

This edition first published in the UK 1992
by Blandford
(a Cassell imprint)
Villiers House
41/47 Strand
LONDON
WC2N 5JE

Distributed in the United States
by Sterling Publishing Co., Inc.
387 Park Avenue South, New York, NY 10016-8810

Distributed in Australia
by Capricorn Link (Australia) Pty Ltd
P.O. Box 665, Lane Cove, NSW 2066

British Library Cataloguing-in-Publication Data.
A catalogue record for this book is available from the
British Library.

ISBN 0-7137-2336-X

Printed and bound in Great Britain by Hollen Street Press

CONTENTS

ABOUT THE AUTHOR

The author of this book, Ken Whitehead, is an all-round fisherman happy with whatever species is found in the water he happens to be fishing. His biggest fish is a pike well in excess of 30lb and he can include carp in the early 20s among the many entries in his fishing diary. He has come to feel that while the pike's lifestyle includes the taking of live fish, the use of livebaiting is not for him.

Ken is also a keen game fisherman and regularly seeks sewin and salmon in Wales as well as trout fishing on many of the southern counties' reservoirs. He is a lone angler who fishes for pleasure, wary of angling politics and distrustful of complicated fishing tackle and over-talkative anglers.

The artist responsible for the clear, no-nonsense drawings is Russell Birkett, who has a BA (Hons) degree in Graphic Information and Design from Falmouth. The illustrations in this book were his first major contribution to the field of book illustration.

Len Cacutt, general editor, has been closely concerned with angling publishing in all its forms, having himself written a number of books and compiled and edited angling books, magazines and encyclopedias for the leading publishers, and was Founder Editor of an angling newspaper.

PART I
RODS AND REELS

For the novice angler, entering a fishing tackle shop early in his career there is before him a vast array of rods of all lengths, colours, sections, with multi-coloured whippings, rod-rings, handles of different lengths in wood, cork, and plastic. In this section of the book, fishing rods are described in terms of materials, construction and action and the kinds of fishing that they are variously designed for.

The reader will learn that the rod chosen must suit the build of its owner and that taper is a vital factor in producing 'action' — how the rod responds in the hands of an angler.

The necessary partner to a rod is a reel and again the choice for the beginner is formidable. The newcomer sees centrepins, fixed-spools both open and closed-face, multipliers all with a wide range of sizes, models and prices. Here, each kind is described and illustrated, with sound advice on the job each one is designed to do.

1 FISHING RODS

INTRODUCTION

There is no such thing as the perfect fishing rod. It can never be made. Every angler who you talk to about rods will eagerly describe to you what in their opinion is the best — but all they are doing is describing the rod which suits *them*. Before you enter a fishing tackle shop to make your choice and buy your first fishing rod you must consider many facts.

First of all there is your particular build. If you are small in stature, a big rod will be cumbersome for you and counter-productive to your fishing; for you it will be awkward. Try to imagine a short person using a long fishing rod and attempting to make a long cast and you will soon see what the problem is. But equally, at the same time a short rod in the hands of a large person can also be a bad investment and prevent the angler from getting the most enjoyment from the sport.

Imagine a 6 ft man using a 5 ft rod to cast with and you can see that he will be wasting energy.

No matter how hard the angler swings the rod, its shortness will be counter-productive to the distance that can be achieved because the leverage will be quite wrong.

There are, however, a few exceptions to this rule and one of them is pole fishing. With these rods, very different from the usual kind, the length of cast is restricted by the length of pole that is being used because the line is attached directly to the pole's tip. To some extent, the second exception is the fly rod, where the weight of line can help influence the distance that can be achieved.

So not only must the rod 'fit' the angler's body, but it must also be capable of coping with the species of fish that are likely to be caught by the angler (1). The somewhat willow-like match-fishing rod with its delicate tip would be completely out of place when being used for pike fishing, where large lures or baits need to be cast, often over a fair distance. Another instance is the rod used for legering, which will naturally be firmer in its action than a general-purpose coarse-fishing rod.

Finally, there is the question of location — where the angler is going to fish. If the fishing is to be on large, open waters, the angler will need a rod capable of casting a bait over considerable distances if the water is to be explored to find the fish and obtain the best-possible sport from it. (2)

But small waters such as streams, tiny ponds, canals and similar restricted expanses will require a much smaller rod altogether, more especially if there are considerable areas overgrown with trees, bushes and so on that will hinder casting. The kind of water and its surroundings can therefore dictate to some extent the best type of rod.

From time to time tackle manufacturers have tried to introduce on to the market rod designs under the description of combination rods. These models will have several middle and end joints which can be combined in a number of permutations which, in theory at least, provide rods to cope with fish varying in size from a gudgeon weighing an ounce to a 50 lb carp.

But the combination rod has never been a success — principally because when it is in use there is little or no feel to whichever combination of sections the angler has selected. 'Feel' is something that is difficult to describe but can best be summed up as that quality in a rod which allows the angler to sense and possibly predict the moves made by a hooked fish from the vibrations transferred up the line to the rod, and then down to the angler's hand.

Try to imagine how a stout pike-rod would feel if it were playing a minnow, or if a pike were

fighting strongly on a thin and floppy fly rod
and you will get a mental picture of rod feel.
(3)

3

The one-rod-for-different-fish idea is not
workable. This means that the angler is going
to need more than one rod if the wish is to
pursue different species of fish, and this (as
usual these days) will entail some extra
expense. But a word of advice: never try to cut

corners by purchasing cheap fishing rods, or any other fishing gear. Buy a good-quality rod, find out how to use it properly, and study and learn one style of fishing before you move on. Also remember that there are sometimes very good second-hand rods on the market from people who have retired from the sport for some reason. These rods are often very cheap indeed and of excellent quality.

Many different kinds of material have gone into the manufacture of rods over the years, and it is useful to know at least something about all of them — especially if the purchase of a second-hand rod is being considered.

Fishing rods were originally formed from wood, using materials such as whole cane, which was excellent for the butt and middle joints of rods where its hollow centre kept weight to a minimum. Greenheart and lancewood were two other woods used, not just for the whole of the rods but for top joints in both coarse and fly rods. Both of these woods are temperamental and likely to snap or split without warning. They also have a tendency to take up a permanent 'set', or curve, if not stored carefully and in the proper way.

For many years split-cane was the king of rod materials, and it is still sought-after and used today. Six lengths are split from a large-sectioned whole cane and then planed into a tapered v-section, the base part of the triangle being formed from the hard outer surface of the cane. The sections are then glued and fitted together to form the complete rod. The finished article is both tough and sensitive, and the feel of a fish being played on a split-cane rod is unique — but such rods are expensive. Like all woods from which rods are made, cane is delicate and liable to become soft, or take a bend that cannot be removed.

Then came the arrival of rods made from a man-made material, glass-fibre, and this largely superseded the rods made from wood. The first models made from glass-fibre were solid in section, but soon the technique of rolling hollow-section rods on mandrels was perfected and glass-fibre was used for all kinds of fishing rods. But though it was tough, glass-fibre was liable to greenstick-type fractures if excessive pressure or strain was placed upon it. (4)

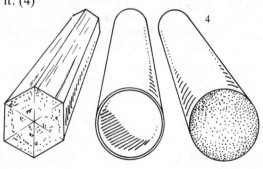

4

Carbon-fibre followed glass-fibre and is now the most widely used rod-forming material. It had a few teething problems — largely centred around its brittleness — but it is now accepted as probably the best material to date. Originally very expensive, it has now dropped greatly in price and rods are available in a range to suit most pockets. More recently boron and even more exotic materials have appeared, but they are expensive and so far confined almost solely to fly-rod manufacture.

Finally, try to remember the following salient facts about fishing rods:

- A rod is merely an extension of the angler's arm. (5)

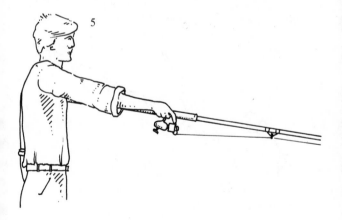

- It helps you cast the bait towards the fish. (6)

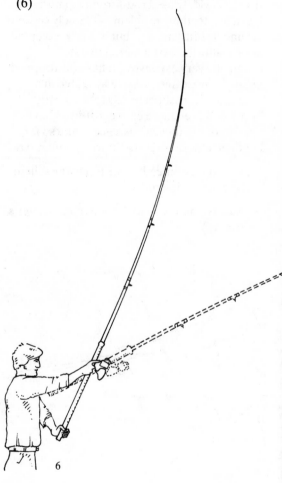

6

■ It helps you make a strike. (7)

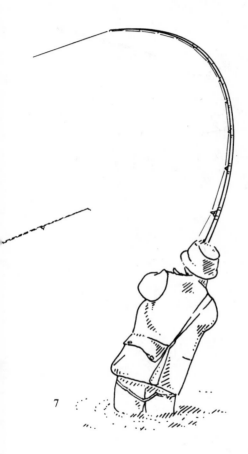

7

- It helps in playing a fish when it has been hooked. (8)

ROD LENGTHS

The specific job that a rod has been designed
to do tends to govern its length and rods fall
into some general categories:

- General fishing and match-fishing rods are
  usually in the 11-13 ft range with three
  joints. (9)

9

- Legering rods tend to be 9 ft or 9 ft 6 in,
  using two joints. (10)

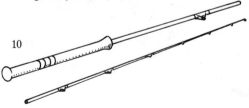

10

- Spinning rods are in two pieces, either around the 10 ft mark for heavy work, or the 7-9 ft length for lighter casting. (11)

11

- Pike fishing rods used to be 5 ft but now are 10 to 11 ft, similar to spinning rods but with a different action. (12)

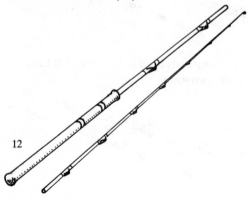

12

- Roach poles vary in length from 15 to 30 ft, sometimes even to 40 ft, and can either be telescopic or be composed of take-apart joints. (13)

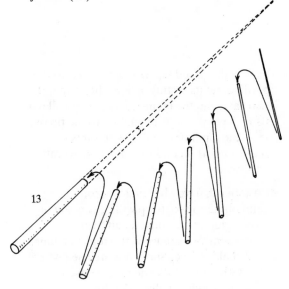

13

TAPER

The way that a rod tapers from its butt to the tip will affect its casting action, the weight that it can cast, and the manner in which it will play a fish. Taper is not just confined to the tip of a rod — the taper in a rod's lower joints is equally important and will affect its overall performance.

- A taper that slowly develops from the butt end of the rod to its tip will be capable of 'springing', or casting, a bait over a considerable distance without it snatching, or breaking free. Such rods are used where heavy baits or tackle need to be used. Spinning rods usually fall in this category. (14)

14

- Taper that commences mainly in the top joint will produce a rod with tip action, used for flicking baits over short distances. Some general coarse-fishing and most match-fishing rods tend to fall in this section. (15)

15

- Some rods are available with what is called a reverse taper. Here the taper starts at the butt end and increases up the rod, then tapers away towards the tip. The advantage of this is in increasing the 'spring' imparted to the bait when it is cast. Usually these rods are used for sea fishing and for pike. (16)

16

- Some match-fishing rods work on the fast-taper principle. Here the taper moves in steps through the length of the rod, making for an action that is very much in the tip — ideal for the fast casting and striking that the matchman requires. (17)

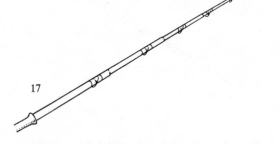

17

ACTION

Naturally, the length of the rod and the taper that it has been given will produce an action that is applicable to that rod alone. Some examples are:

- A long, light rod with a slow taper, which will have a soft action. (18)

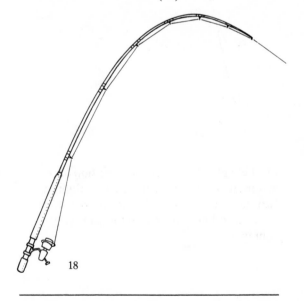

18

- A short rod with little taper in the bottom joints but a steep taper in the top joint will have what is called a tip action. (19)

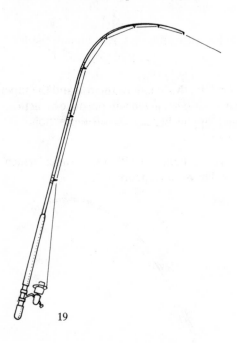

19

(To help generalise in the description of rod action, tackle manufacturers have adopted two standards. One applies to coarse fishing rods, the other to rods used for game (fly) fishing.)

- Coarse fishing rods have their action
  measured by means of a test curve. A simple
  way to understand this is to tie a length of
  line to the tip ring of the rod, and attach this
  to the hook on a spring balance. The rod is
  held vertical and the spring balance pulled
  sideways until the tip of the rod is bent to an
  angle of 90 degrees. At this angle the weight
  is read from the balance, and the reading
  used to describe the rod action. This might
  vary from a few ounces (a light rod) to 1½
  lb. (20)

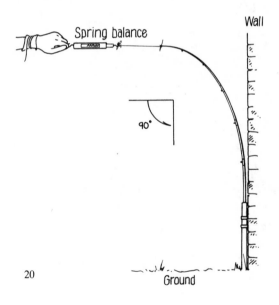

Spring balance

Wall

90°

20

Ground

■ The Association of Fishing Tackle
Manufacturers (AFTM) measures action in
rods used for fly fishing by the number-sign
#. This number refers to the weight of line
that will best work with the rod and from it
comes a simple guide. Generally #4 to 6
rods are for light work — streams and so
on, #7 and 8 for general river and light
reservoir work, and #9 and above for work
that involves heavy duty casting such as
handling heavy weighted fly lines for
reservoir or salmon fishing on big rivers.
(21)

21

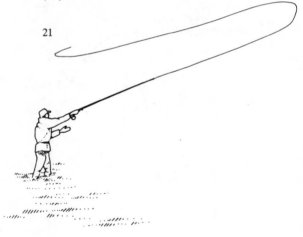

JOINTS

The sections of wooden rods are fastened together by the use of brass fittings called ferrules, named (for obvious reasons) male and female, to either end of each joint. Occasionally they are found in rods made from solid glass-fibre. (22)

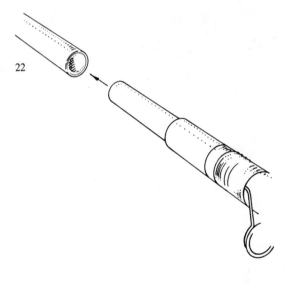

22

■ Hollow-glass and carbon-fibre rods are
connected by spigots, which are formed by
a solid tubular spigot fixed to form the male
mounting at one joint end, into which the
hollow end of the joint above can slide.
Strong and light, these joints rarely give
trouble. (23)

23

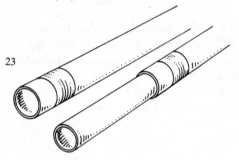

FITTINGS

The two essential fittings to a rod are its handle, and the rod rings which guide and control the line. Both are important items and their position and style will influence the action of the rod.

Handles

- Rod handles are either single (short) or double (long) handed. Single-handed rods are usually found on fly rods, and short rods used for spinning. (24)

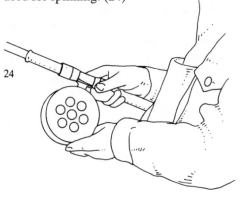

24

■ Double handles are used on longer rods,
the extra length of handle providing comfort
besides the leverage that assists in
developing the cast and in playing a fish.
(25)

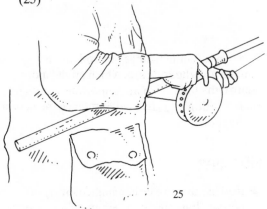

25

■ Handles are either formed from cork, wood
or plastic. Whichever material forms the
handle of your rod, keep it clean and free of
slime and grease by using a little liquid soap
on a clean cloth
when you get
home. (26)

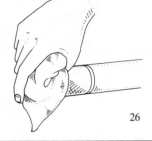

26

Rod Rings

- For float fishing, rod rings are usually of the 'stand off' type, the rings soldered to tall legs that will hold the line away from the rod. This is important — especially when rain tends to make nylon line cling to the rod's surface. The best rings are manufactured from stainless steel, and are either of satin chrome or black chrome to prevent glare. (27)

27

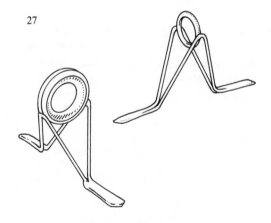

- Rings for rods that have to cope with heavy and powerful fish such as carp and pike, and spinning rods, have heavier rings, generally lined with a material that will not wear and form grooves as the line constantly passes through them. Quality is always something you will have to pay for — the price will be reflected in the rod. (28)

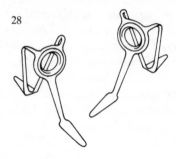

28

■ Butt and end rings — the first and last rings on the rod — take the most wear. On good-quality rods these will have lined rings, and the tip ring will possess legs on either side to prevent line wrapping round and jamming. (29)

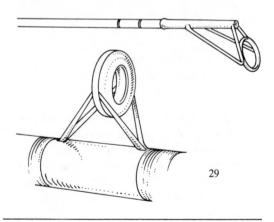

29

CHOOSING A ROD

Before you commit yourself to parting with money for a rod, try to borrow one from a friend. By trying a variety of rods in different angling situations you will soon decide what you like, and dislike. (30) Keep in mind that there is no such thing as an all-round rod — decide what fish you are going to try to catch and look for a rod that will cope with those species. A match-fishing rod is of little use on a fast river like the Hampshire Avon where large fish are going to require some firm

30

handling. Conversely, a stiff, general-purpose rod will be the wrong one if you intend to take up match-fishing. When you are in the tackle shop, look carefully at the quality and finish of the rods. A dark model with matt finish, quality rod rings and a well-finished handle will look and fish like a thoroughbred. Those with chrome strips, flash whippings and garish-coloured joints are designed to attract the angler; they will soon lose their shine.

- **General-purpose float rods.** These have a slow action that produces a bend through a great deal of their length. They will cope with lines up to 5 lb or so in breaking strain, and can handle most situations from long-trotting for chub to tench and light carp fishing. They possess sliding winch fittings that push together over the reel saddle and hold it in place. (31)

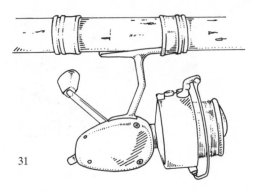

31

■ **Match-fishing rods.** These are fast-
actioned, the taper occurring only in the
end 25 per cent of the rod which allows for
objective casting and fast striking on a bite.
As with general-purpose float rods they are
equipped with sliding winch fittings. (32)

32

■ **Leger rods.** Shorter — 9 to 9 ft 6 in —
these rods have a moderate action allowing
some firm casting but they retain sensitivity
which will enable a bite to be seen by the
angler. To aid this the rod's tip-ring will be
fitted with the means of using a swingtip,
springtip or quivertip. (33, 34, 35)
Swingtips are aids to detecting a bite and
are screwed into the top ring of the rod or
fastened to a spigot by a piece of valve
rubber. The swingtip is best used on
stillwaters where there is no flow and is
most successful when it hangs at an angle of
90 degrees. *Springtips* have a coiled spring
and wire to register bites. *Quivertips* are
short, stiff extensions which screw into the

Leger rod in action

33

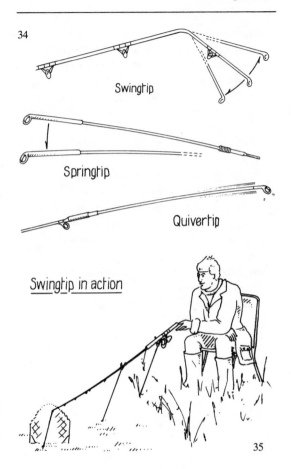

34

Swingtip

Springtip

Quivertip

Swingtip in action

35

end ring of the rod, and register the slightest
move from a fish. Painted with bright
colours they are very effective when used
on moving waters.

■ **Spinning rods.** These fall into two
categories — single and double handed.
The double-handed rod will be from 9 to 10
ft long, with a test curve of 1½ to 2¼ lb, and
possess a slow action which will enable it to
handle sizable baits. The reel fittings will be
screw actioned, allowing the reel to be
clamped firmly to the butt, unable to work
free with the constant casting that will take
place. Single-handed spinning rods, used on
small waters or from boats, are in the 6 to 8
ft range (36). Originally introduced into this
country from the US they are known as
baitcasting rods, and are designed to be
used with a multiplying reel. To help control
the line, a true baitcasting rod has a cranked
handle into which the reel clips. With this
feature it is possible to cast continuously

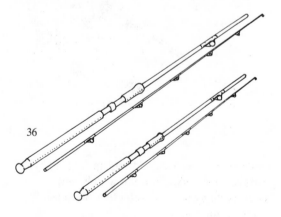

36

and without fatigue throughout the day, allowing the angler to cover a lot of water. (37)

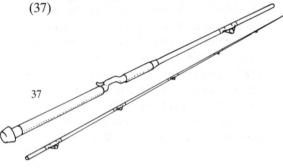

37

■ **Carp rods.** There are many special rods on the market, some of which have been designed by famous anglers and which are capable of handling very large carp. They tend to be in the 11 ft range with a test curve of 1½ lb, handling a line of 6-12 lb breaking strain and are capable of making long casts that are often necessary to get a bait to the fish. (38)

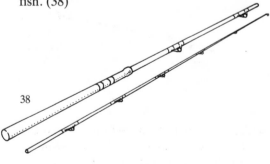

38

- **Pike rods.** These operate best when they
  have fast-taper blanks with a test curve in
  the 2¼ to 2½ lb range and when the angler
  is using small baits. But for long-range
  casting with heavy baits a slow-action rod
  will be better. There are many specialist
  pike rods sporting well known names in the
  tackle shops. Some anglers have been
  known to use light sea fishing beachcasters
  on very large waters, where baits have to be
  cast over a long distance. (39)

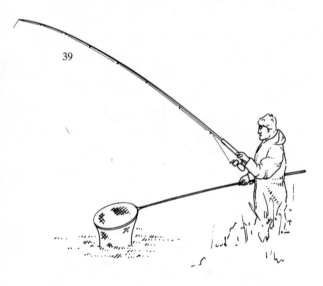

39

- **Poles.** Originally made from hollow cane
  and used exclusively on the Thames and
  Lea for roach, the pole is now one of the

chief weapons in the match-angler's armoury and is used on waters throughout the country and on the Continent. Generally poles vary in length from 15 to 30 ft, and the more you pay then the better they are. For the best poles you can pay up to £1,000. Their advantage is that they enable complete line control and keep the rod tip on top of the float, ready to deal with the most sensitive of bites. The alloy crook and length of elastic allow some give in playing a fish — quite a big consideration when there is no reel, the line being attached to the top of the rod. (40, 41)

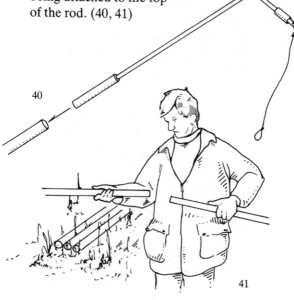

40

41

LOOKING AFTER RODS

Rods never wear out. The rings may become worn, and the varnish scuffed — but rods usually fail because they have been neglected or damaged in some way. One of the first things to remember is that a rod must be kept in its case, which will keep all the joints together. To keep them safely when not in use they should be hung by the loop at the bag end in the dry. (42)

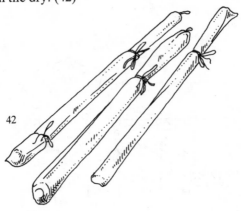

42

■ After use, wipe and dry your rods when you get home. Damp working its way under the rod whippings is one of the quickest ways of losing a rod ring — just at the wrong moment. (43)

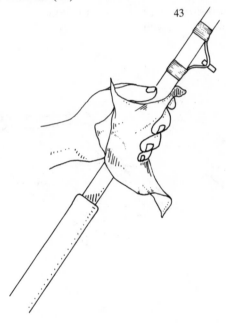

43

■ Pay special attention to the handle. Clean it with a little washing-up liquid and rinse and dry thoroughly.

■ When going fishing it pays to carry your
  rods in a holdall, which not only keeps them
  together but also gives added protection
  against knocks. Several types are on the
  market, either as tubes or roll-up models.
  Choose one large enough to take an
  umbrella as well. (44)

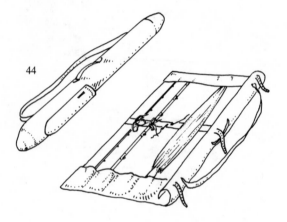

44

ROD REPAIRS

There is not much that can go wrong with the modern fishing rod, but there are two areas of wear that will occur and which will need attention. But don't panic, these are well within the angler's grasp.

- When spigots wear, the ends of the two joints butt together. This will loosen them and the rod joint will separate when you cast. The cure is to take a medium file and gently remove a little from off the female joint end. (45)

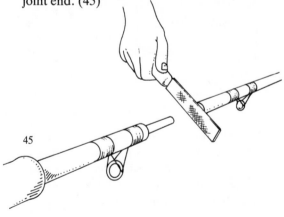

45

- Carry out the filing a little at a time and constantly check the fit. If you take too much off, the joints won't fit together, and if you have planned a fishing trip for the next day you will have a problem.

- Damaged rod whippings (sometimes called wrappings) should be repaired as soon as possible. Your tackle dealer will be able to sell you a reel of whipping material to match that which needs replacing. You will also need cellulose varnish and some ordinary rod varnish — also available at the tackle dealer. (46)

46
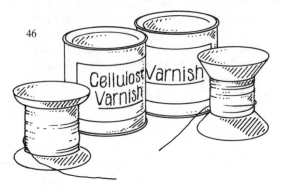

- Start by removing the ring from the rod and cleaning off old varnish and whipping and gently rubbing the area with extra fine glass paper until it is smooth. Then use sticky tape to hold the ring in place. (47)

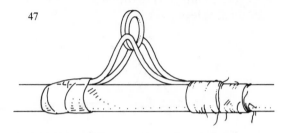

47

- Trap one end of the whipping by taking a full turn round the rod below the platform of the rod ring, then commence winding it on, keeping each turn tight against the next one. (48)

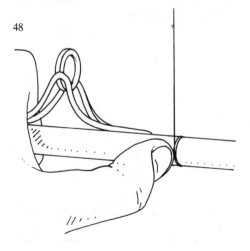

48

- Carry on until you are within 9 or 10 turns of the ring legs. (49)

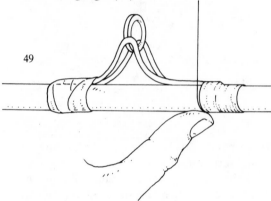

49

- Then fold a short length of thread and carry on whipping over this. (50)

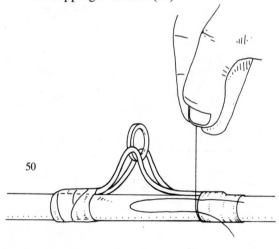

50

- Thread the whipping end through the loop, and pull it back till it lies under the whipping. (51)

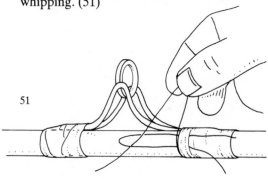

51

- Hold the end free, and cut with a razor blade. (52)

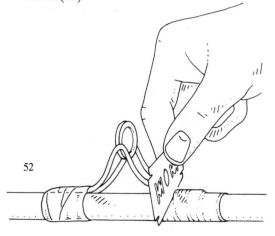

52

- Flood the whipping with several coats of cellulose varnish until the grooves between the whippings are filled. (53)

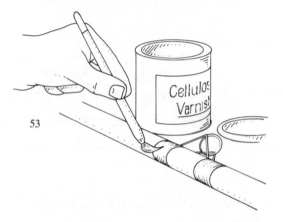

- When dry, give two coats of rod varnish, leaving to dry in a dust-free place and the job is done. (54)

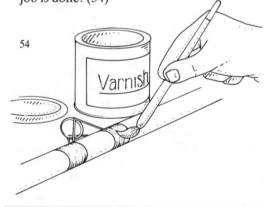

2 REELS

INTRODUCTION

Put into simple terms, a reel exists merely to store line without it tangling until the angler is ready to release it, or to retrieve it. No matter how many levers or gears a reel has it can carry out nothing other than these two operations and there is no guarantee that reels which are designed to have several different types of control over the line are any better than the more simple models. (55)

55

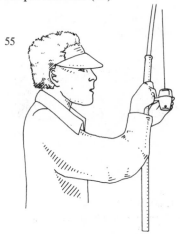

CHOOSING A REEL

The most important thing to look for when selecting a reel is the material from which it has been made, together with the degree of engineering skill and technique that has gone into its design and manufacture. Soft metal, poorly engineered gears and badly sited handles or control levers will make using the reel a nightmare instead of the natural aid that it should be. (56)

56

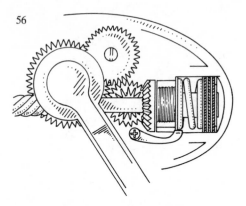

Parting with good money usually ensures that the reel has been made from good-quality metal or, more recently, carbon fibre. It will give a life-time of service — providing that it is looked after. As with selecting a rod, the angler should be careful when he makes his choice of fishing reel. It is essential that the reel should suit the type of fishing to be undertaken, the type of water where it is to be fished, and the species of fish that are to be sought.

Further, the angler must consider that the reel must match the rod he is going to use. This matching together of rod and reel, called balance, is all-important. It is not just size that matters — weight must also be taken into consideration, especially if, for instance, the angler is going to spin — something that will necessitate his holding the rod and casting for most of the day. (57)

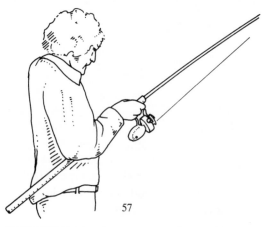

57

There are three types of reel from which the angler can choose, the centrepin reel, the fixed-spool reel and the multiplying reel. Each have their merits and their uses. Before purchasing either of the basic types, try to use one belonging to a friend. (58)

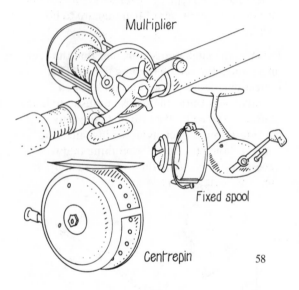

Multiplier

Fixed spool

Centrepin   58

Some reels can be difficult to cope with — for instance, many anglers never manage to get the hang of using a multiplying reel. Persevere and practise — but if you cannot become accustomed to using a particular type of reel, leave it alone. Above all — never just buy a reel simply for its appearance.

Centrepin Reels

Basically, a centrepin is a flanged drum which revolves in a close fitting backplate, and the centrepin reel has been in use since anglers needed to store line. The drum revolves in parallel with the rod handle, line feeding directly from the drum into the first rod ring.

- With no angles for the line to follow, this leads to great control and sensitivity. Easy to maintain, the best centrepins cost money — you are paying for the machining of both drum and body — but with only one moving part, there is little wear and a reel will last a lifetime. The principal use of the centrepin is for long-trotting, the current of the river taking float and bait downstream and pulling line straight from the drum while allowing the angler to concentrate on possible bites. Naturally this free-running action is only possible from reels made of light alloy — wooden reels (often called Nottingham reels) and some old Bakelite or plastic ones have a drum too heavy to be moved by the end tackle. Some centrepin models have a drag system fitted which prevents line being stripped so quickly that the reel over-runs, causing what is called a 'bird's nest' around the drum. Usually there is a check that can be switched over by means of a lever — something useful when playing a fish. (59)

59

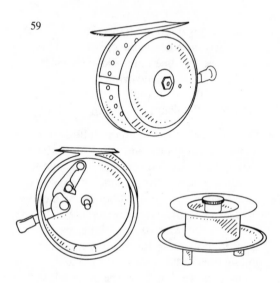

■ Because the reel is so free-running there is no need to wind line back onto the drum by the handles on the side of the case. Instead the line is 'batted' by tapping with the fingers on the rim of the drum. The careful positioning of the thumb prevents an overrun on the retrieve. (60)

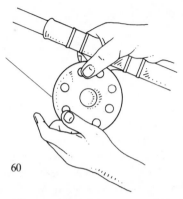

60

■ Out of favour for a number of years, the centrepin is making a comeback with many anglers — especially the matchmen — who appreciate the direct control between reel, line and fish, without the gears and springs that are used on other models. When filling the reel the line is wound onto the spool directly, using some tension – it is better that someone holds the spooled line otherwise line trapping will occur on the drum. (61)

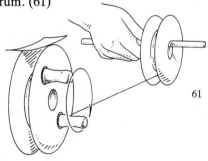

61

Fixed-Spool Reels

Originally called threadline reels — so-named because they used ordinary sewing thread as line — fixed-spool reels have been one of the many revolutions in the angling world. With the aid of a fixed-spool reel it is possible to cast over considerable distances effortlessly, and without line tangle.

■ This largely relates to the fact that the drum of the reel is at right angles to the rod handle and line is pulled free over the lip of the reel. The drum does not revolve, as in the centrepin model. (62)

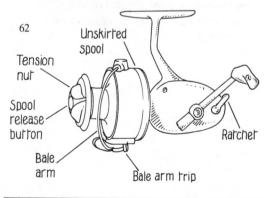

62

Unskirted spool

Tension nut

Spool release button

Bale arm

Bale arm trip

Ratchet

■ Another advantage of the fixed-spool reel is
that the angler has a clutch between the
handle and spool, allowing the line to slip
when excessive pull takes place — i.e.,
when playing a strong-fighting fish. This
clutch can be adjusted by using the tension
nut usually placed at the front of the reel, in
front of the drum. There are, however,
models where the drag adjustment is by
means of a knob placed behind the body of
the reel; an advantage of this positioning is
the fact that tension can be adjusted while a
fish is being played.

The first fixed-spool reels had an unskirted
spool, which allowed line to slip to the rear of
the back of the spool and catch on the spindle
behind. To avoid this the skirted spool was
designed to overcome this difficulty. (63)

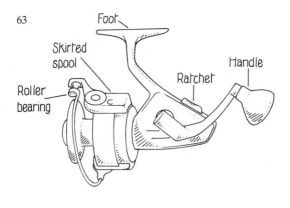

63

Different gearing on the reel will offer varying rates of retrieve. The normal ratio is 4 to 1, providing a retrieve rate of about 16 in to one turn of the handle.

Line snagging is a problem with any reel — especially when it is windy, or the angler is fishing from banks that are obstructed with undergrowth. To deal with this problem, the tackle manufacturers' designed the closed-face reel.

Closed-Face Reels

Here all mechanism, such as the bale arm around which line fits, is completely covered by a shield. Line is released by pressing a button at the front of the spool, and it will begin retrieval on the first rotation of the handle. The clutch is adjusted by means of a tension knob fitted to the handle, at the junction with the spool. (64)

64

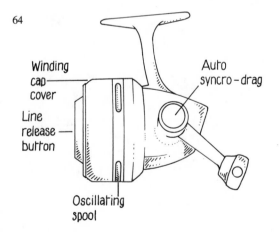

Winding cap cover

Line release button

Auto syncro-drag

Oscillating spool

■ These reels are only as good as the engineering in them — so you should buy the best you can afford. There is an inbuilt disadvantage with the fixed-spool reel, and that is line twist or kink. Care must be taken when loading the spool. The revolving action of the bale arm around the spool puts a kink into a line being wound directly onto it — the normal method. Instead, the spool from which line is drawn should be held parallel to the drum of the reel, and line drawn off over its lip, in the same manner that line leaves the reel during a cast. Take care to fill the spool with line to within ⅛ of an inch of the lip. If this is not done, drag will occur as line is pulled over the lip, and the length of the line will be restricted. (65, 66)

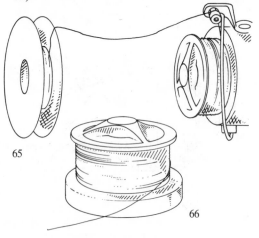

65

66

Multiplying Reels

Multiplying reels, or 'multipliers', are reels
that possess a small-diameter drum geared to a
ratio of 3 or 4 to 1, so producing a very rapid
retrieve of the line. There is a wide variety of
this kind of reel on the market, some of the
up-to-date models possessing magnetic drags,
oil drag retarders and automatic gearing.

■ A good multiplier will have centrifugal
braking — as the cast progresses so friction
pads will slow the drum to prevent over-run.
There will also be an automatic line
spreader to prevent line piling on one area
of the spool, thereby trapping it. (67)

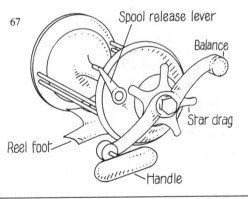

67

■ Multiplying reels are different in that they
are fished with the reel above the rod handle
and not below, in the traditional position.
These reels are capable of allowing a sizable
bait to be punched out for a very long
distance, and coping with big fish —
principally through the direct line taken
from reel to rod tip. This is unlike the fixed-
spool reel where line goes at an angle
through the bale arm, then back through
the angle of the butt ring. Line is loaded
onto the spool of the multiplier directly, in
the same way as the centrepin reel. (68)

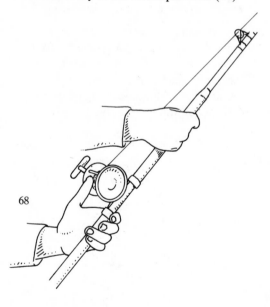

68

- The disadvantages of the multiplying reel lie in their vulnerability to grit and dirt — this can jam them or damage the delicate mechanism inside the end plates — and in unskilled hands they have a tendency to encounter over-runs that produce massive birds' nests. Those anglers who have mastered them swear by them — those who don't, swear at them. The best are expensive but with care they will last a lifetime.

LOOKING AFTER REELS

Dirt, dust and pieces of the angler's bait are a reel's worst enemies. When you buy your reel buy a reel case for it at the same time — there are several varieties on the market, made in sizes to suit every reel. When not in use, keep the reel cased. (69)

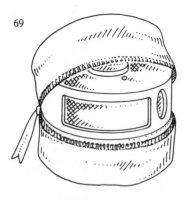

69

- When you return from a fishing trip, take your reels from their cases and let the cases dry thoroughly. Dry the reel too and then strip it down, removing the drum/spool

from the body and cleaning with a dry cloth.
(70)

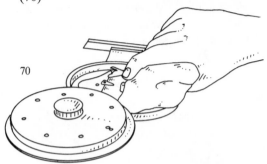

70

■ Reels for freshwater fishing that have been
used in salt or brackish water should
immediately be washed in fresh water, then
dried. Some metals used in freshwater-reel
manufacture will corrode
quickly if salt is left
adhering. (71)

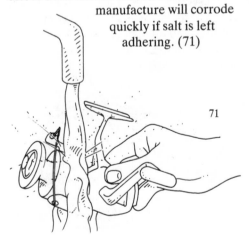

71

■ When dry, wipe the reel body and spool back with a cloth on which a little oil (WD 40 or similar) has been sprayed. Then pack the reel in its case ready for use again. Be careful not to get oil on any monofilament line. (72)

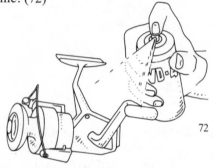

72

■ At least once during a season — more with constant use — reels should be completely stripped and oiled or greased. This is especially important in the case of fixed-spool and multiplying reels. (73)

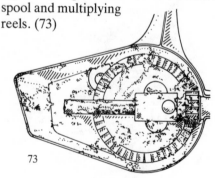

73

- Brush and work Swarfega or any similar recommended grease-remover into the body of the reel with a brush to dissolve stale grease and dirt. (74)

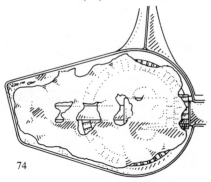

74

- Wash under a tap and dry. (75)

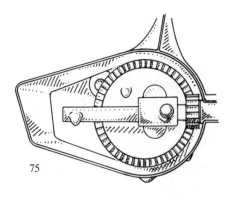

75

■ Re-pack with grease — your tackle shop
will sell the right type for your reel. (76)

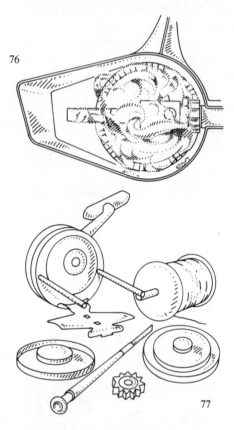

76

77

■ Take special care when dealing with
multiplying reels. Study the manufacturer's
guide before stripping — and do the job on

a table laid with white paper as a background. There are often tiny springs, screws and so on in these reels which can easily be lost. Take special care to use the lubricant recommended by the manufacturer when re-assembling. (77)

■ Avoid packing line tightly onto a reel. Each time you get snagged and pull to get free, line with be pulled hard and tight onto the reel, so tightening into the line already stored. If you repeat this several times during an outing, pressure can be caused that will jam folds of line one under the other or, worse, the spool may be distorted and unable to revolve. Always pull line above the tip ring to free a snag, wrapping it round your clothed forearm (not a finger) and taking a straight strain. (78)

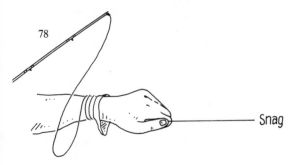

78

Snag

BALANCING ROD AND REEL

Balance is all important when rod and reel are joined together. Imagine holding something that is either tip heavy or butt heavy for around eight hours and you will get some idea of how tiring and unpleasant it can be. (79)

79

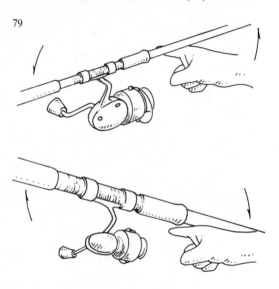

■ Ideally both reel and rod should balance.
   The point of balance is taken as just above
   the handle and it is worth going to great
   lengths to achieve this when putting rod and
   reel together. (80)

80

CASTING TECHNIQUES

Even the best-balanced rod and reel need some know-how from the angler if they are to get the bait where it is wanted. Casting comes with practice, but there is no need to practise at the waterside. Without a hook, casting can be practised in a field and those determined to reach the top in angling — especially match anglers — are not frightened to do so. There are several types of cast, the most universally used in bottom fishing being the overhead cast. The following sequence shows how it may be done.

- Space your hands well apart on the rod handle and keep the rod tip vertical with the float hanging a few feet or so below the tip ring. (81)

- Move the rod backwards over the shoulder until the tip is angled at about 45 degrees. (82)

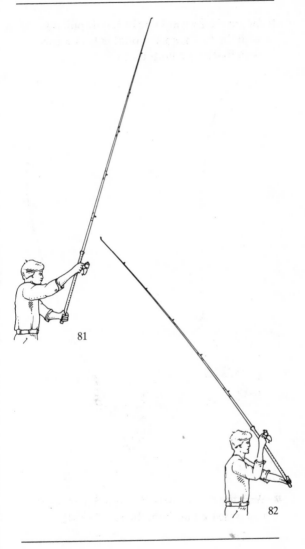

81

82

- Begin the forward stroke boldly pulling
  with the top hand and pulling backwards
  with that at the bottom. (83)

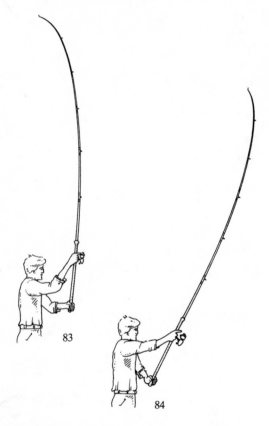

- With the rod around 45 degrees in front of
  you, release line from the reel — (84)

- and hold the rod down, allowing the line to follow through as the bait and float are taken away. (85)

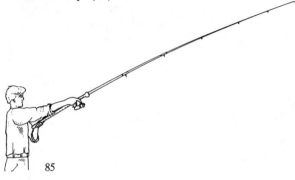

85

- When the bait hits the water keep the rod tip down, and above the surface of the water. (86)

86

Underarm Casting

■ The rod is held in front of the angler, line above the hook in one hand and the finger of the other hand braking the reel, preventing line pulling free. (87)

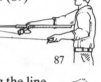

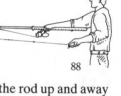

87

■ Spring the rod tip by pulling the line back — (88)

88

■ and release it, swinging the rod up and away so that the bait and float shoot out over the water. (89, 90)

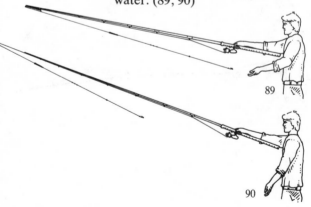

89

90

Bait Casting — The Overhead Cast

- A technique for those spinning with the single handed rod.

- Swing the bait up and backwards over your head. (91)

91

- Allow the weight of the bait to flex the rod back — (92)

92

- then force the rod tip forward, throwing the bait forward. (93)

93

- Keep the rod tip down to allow line to follow through. (94)

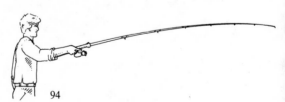

94

PLAYING A FISH

When a sizable fish is hooked remember that cool and determined action will bring it to the net. Snatching in a panic will surely lose anything but the smallest tiddler. (95)

95

■ While the fish is running and in safe water, i.e. without snags, the fish can have its head — but with resistance from the angler either from the drag on a fixed-spool reel or on the rim of the drum on a centrepin reel. (96)

96

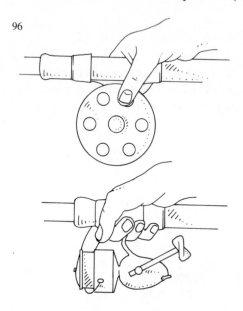

■ When the fish runs into possible cover such as weed beds or overhanging bushes where a break may occur, use side strain to turn its head and alter its direction. Never point the rod towards the fish; keep it at an angle which will allow the spring in the rod to help tire the catch out. (97)

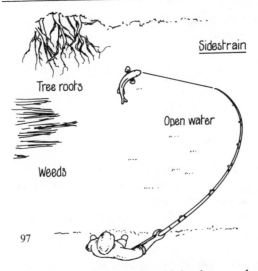

Sidestrain

Tree roots

Open water

Weeds

97

- When the fish tires, 'pump' it back towards you by alternately raising the rod tip and recovering line until it is within range of the landing net. (98)

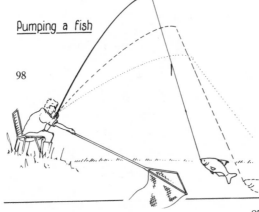

Pumping a fish

98

■ Sink the net and draw the fish gently over it. (99)

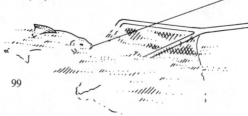

99

■ Lift rod and landing net together when the fish is well enveloped, and take it well back up the bank, away from the water. One last tip: always unhook your fish while it is still in the net. If you remove it from the meshes before unhooking it might give a sudden jump and be away, and it might have been that very good specimen you have been trying for for ages! (100)

100

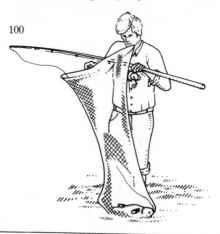

PART II
HOOKS, LINES AND KNOTS

Young Huckleberry Finn used string and a bent pin when he went trying for catfish. But while a feeding fish is not aware of the difference between the pin and a modern machine-made hook, Huck's chances would have been very much improved!

Above the hook the line carries floats, weights and swivels – and then leads through the rod rings to the reel. Some of these items need knots for attachment but when tied in nylon knots can spell danger, for nylon is notorious in that knots slip easily. So the author runs through knots used most often by anglers and known to hold under stress.

Until recently, lead split shot was the universal method of weighting floats to ensure that they were sensitive and correctly balanced. But then it was claimed that discarded lead shot was responsible for poisoning swans. Now, legislation is in force banning the use of lead for angling use below a certain weight, and all references to split shot and shotting patterns refer to the various commercially produced lead substitutes.

It is obvious that fish see below the surface, assuming of course that the water is clear and not thick with suspended matter. But fish can also see through the surface film, although here their vision is to some extent distorted. So great care should be taken when it comes to the selection and presentation of terminal tackle. The items of which it is composed may cost little when compared with the price of a new rod or reel. They are called terminal tackle because they are literally at the end of the line — and the angler really has to know just what he should, and should not do if he is going to hook his fish. In this section of the book there are three items that we must consider in connection with the angler's terminal tackle: hooks, line — and knots; the means of joining the two together.

3 HOOKS

INTRODUCTION

Without doubt, hooks are the most important item in the angler's tackle box. This basic element of the angler's tackle dates back thousands of years to the Stone Age. Hooks made from flint and bone are known from those times and they have barbs and points very similar to today's machine-made ones (1).

1

4000 year old
hook from late
Stone Age
made of bone

Modern hook

Unless the hook is reliable there is a possibility that the fish will either fail to be hooked, or it will break free. There is a bewildering display of hooks on the market and many of them are described later in this book, but at first the angler should concentrate on a few of the standard models available, leaving the purchase of those that are for specialist purposes until they are required.

For most of his time at the waterside the coarse fisherman will be using single hooks tied to the end of his line. There are also other kinds of hooks available that are welded together either as double or as treble hooks. These are usually used on spinning lures and on plugs. (2)

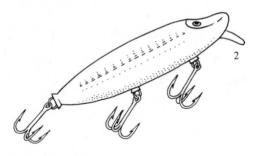

Occasionally hooks are mounted one above the other as an aid to carrying a bait in such a way that it can easily be seen by fish. The Pennell tackle is one such method, where two hooks are tied to the line one above the other in what is described as tandem style. Another method, using three hooks, is called Stewart tackle. (3)

3

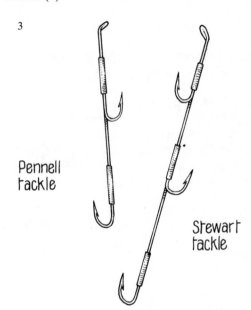

Pennell
tackle

Stewart
tackle

HOOK ANATOMY

The majority of fishing hooks are mass-
produced by machine from wire. It is
important that this wire must have a good
temper, which means that it should not bend
out of shape easily, and that it should be thin.
Testing the temper of a hook is best carried
out by holding it by the shank and pulling just
above the point with a pair of fine pliers. There
should be give, but no straightening. (4)

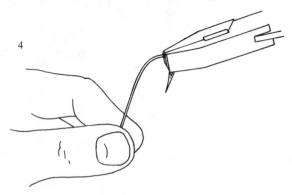

4

- The various parts of a hook have names,
  and it is better to understand the technical
  terms that are used — especially if you are
  trying to describe something in a tackle

shop. The diagram here describes the various parts. (5)

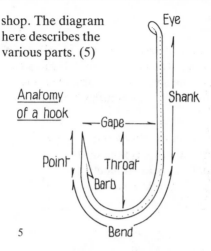

Anatomy of a hook

Eye

Shank

Gape

Point

Throat

Barb

Bend

5

- Hooks that must have extra strength — those used for really powerful fish such as large pike and salmon — are not produced from wire, but are forged from heavy metal, which means they are not often used in general float fishing, but have applications when the angler is freelining a bait which is intended to be taken as it sinks, or lies on the bottom. Carp fishermen find these hooks useful. (6)

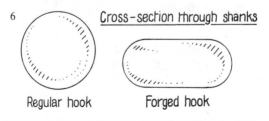

6   Cross-section through shanks

Regular hook   Forged hook

Bends

The bend of the hook (see Pic. 5) will affect the way that a bait is presented. It can also influence the direction in which the hook is lodged into the fish's mouth when the angler strikes.

- The Limerick bend has a sharp angle and is regarded by many as being difficult for a fish to release itself from. (7)

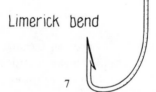

Limerick bend

7

- Much favoured by the coarse angler for worm fishing the round bend has a wide gape which connects easily with the mouth. (8)

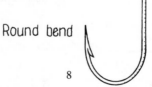

Round bend

8

- A bend called the Viking (a manufacturer's trade name) is sharp-angled and turns back towards the shank (see Pic. 5). This helps prevent a fish from breaking free. (9)

Viking bend

9

- Most popular in coarse fishing, the simple crystal bend is used universally, especially when maggot is the bait, either singly or in a bunch. (10)

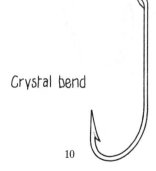

Crystal bend

10

■ The Model Perfect is a round bend with a
  slightly off-set point developed by the
  manufacturers Allcocks. It is a design from
  which many other hooks were developed.
  The bends of hooks are not only measured
  in relation to the gape — they are also
  measured in relation to the angle with the
  shank of the hook. (11)

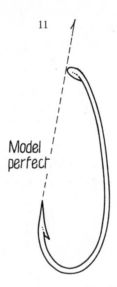

11

Model
perfect

■ The straight bend. Here the point runs in line with the shank of the hook. (12)

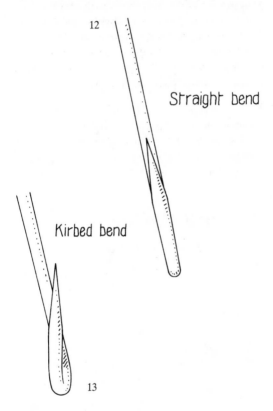

■ Kirbed bend — where the point is set to the right, out of line with the shank. This is favoured by many as being an aid in driving the hook home on the strike. (13)

Points

Making the entry into the mouth of the fish, a point must be sharp, well shaped and fine. If thick, clumsy and blunt it won't penetrate the mouth area — especially in those species of fish that have a large and well-developed bone structure in the jaws, such as pike.

- Barbless points are favoured by the match angler where it is easy to unhook a fish, thus saving time. The angler must maintain a tight line all the time he is playing a fish on a barbless hook if it is not to be lost. (14)

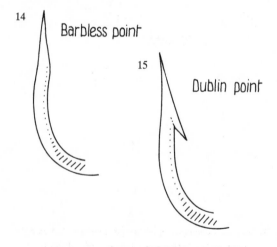

14 Barbless point

15 Dublin point

- Dublin points curve out, away from the shank of the hook. (15)

- Curved-in points have a curve towards the shank of the hook. (16)

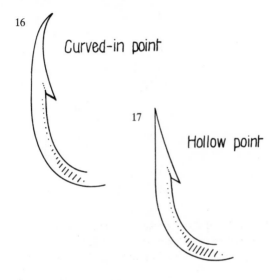

- Hollow point hooks have a straight outer edge. (17)

Barbs

The smallest part of a hook, yet the most important by far and one that frequently gives trouble. Always check the barb on every new hook that you use — there is often a dud one in a batch.

- A barb deeply cut into the metal will weaken the hook. (18)

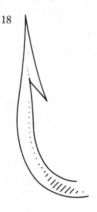

- Barbs set too far back from the point are difficult to drive home — and can snap off or break the line as the angler strikes. (19)

Eyes

On a hook, the means whereby a hook can be attached to the line. Always find the hook with the smallest eyes you can. The bigger the eye, the bigger the risk of the hook hanging sloppily at an angle to the line, or the line riding round the eye and weakening the nylon. Ideally, the line should just fit comfortably through the eye, neither too tight nor too loose.

■ Tapered eyes. These are the most widely used eyes, and the curve should be complete, the end of the circle touching the shank of the hook so that line cannot slip free. (20)

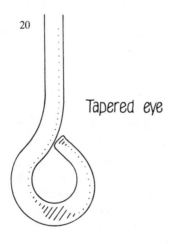

20

Tapered eye

- Ball eyes. These are similar to tapered eyes, but there is no taper in the diameter of the wire. Again, make sure that the ball is closed, or line may slip free. (21)

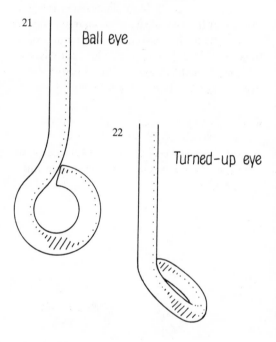

21 Ball eye

22 Turned-up eye

- Turned up eyes. The eye of the hook turns away from the point — an aid to hooking that some anglers insist on. Turned down eyes have the eye turning in towards the point, frequently found on hooks used for trout flies. (22)

- Double eyes. As the name suggests, these are found on double hooks — the eye turns away from the points. (23)

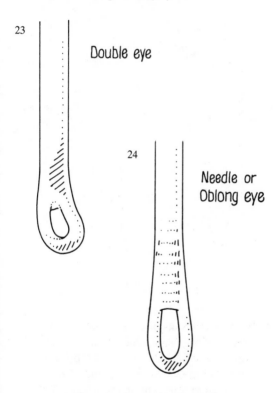

- Needle or oblong eyes are standard on treble hooks, allowing them to be whipped to traces or mounted to spoons or plugs. (24)

- Looped eyes are usually found on heavy hooks, especially in salmon fishing. The loop is turned up. (25)

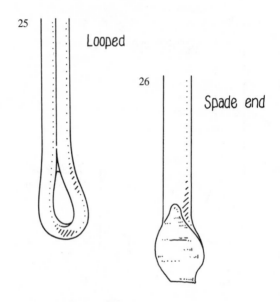

- Spade-end hooks have flattened shanks instead of the usual eye, which allows the angler to tie his line direct onto the hook below the shank. In this position the line cannot slide free. The spade-end hook is widely used by coarse fishermen, especially the match angler, because the position of the knot on the shank ensures the point being driven upwards in a straight line. (26)

Shanks

The shank of the hook can affect the angle of penetration at its point. Generally the longer the shank is in relation to the eye, the smaller its angle of penetration must be. This means that the hook goes in easily but not very far. On the other hand the short shanked hook needs a more powerful strike to drive it home, but it will penetrate more deeply.

- The bait which is to be used should govern the length of shank. Cereals, worms, sweetcorn and similar baits need a hook with a long shank. Maggots should be used on a short-shanked hook. (27)

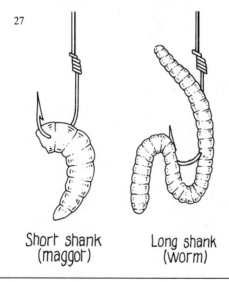

27

Short shank
(maggot)

Long shank
(worm)

■ Sliced shanks on hooks have a barb
  designed to stop bait from slipping down
  onto the bend and are often used in sea
  fishing, but they also have a use for the
  freshwater angler. Sliced shanks can be
  purchased in small sizes. (28)

28

Sliced shank

Ready-Tied Hooks

Sold in packets, ready-tied hooks are attached
to a length of nylon which has a loop at the
other end so that it can be tied directly to the
reel line. The nylon is machine-whipped to the
hook, and not tied with a knot, the fine
whipping being varnished to prevent wear and
provide strength. As with most items of fishing
tackle, the more you pay, the better will be the
quality and hooks-to-nylon are no exception.
(29)

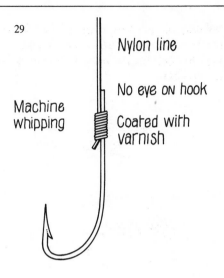

29

Nylon line

No eye on hook

Machine
whipping

Coated with
varnish

Multiple Hooks

Double and treble hooks are usually mounted
on spinners and plugs, which are used for
catching predatory fish including pike, perch,
salmon and trout and so on. (30)

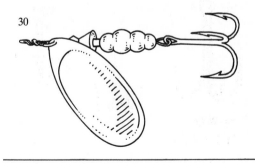

30

■ Salmon flies are frequently tied on double
hooks, the extra weight of two hooks
together helping the fly to sink in very fast
water. (31)

31

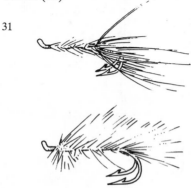

■ Treble hooks should be formed from fine
wire whenever small lures are being used.
Heavy, clumsy trebles can totally ruin the
spinning action of a delicate lure. (32)

32

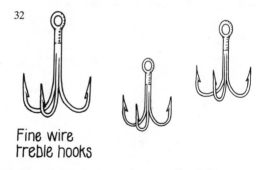

Fine wire
treble hooks

■ As with single hooks, trebles have sizes with the lower the number the larger the hook. A round bend is usual — there are alternatives, but rarely used. Look for a good, bronzed finish which will not rust. (33)

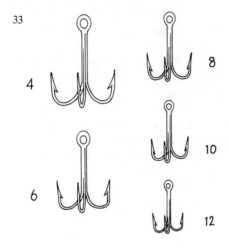

33

4

8

6

10

12

CHOOSING HOOKS

Only the best possible hook quality should be good enough, regardless of the price. When you are in the tackle shop buy your hooks by the box, but first ask to be allowed carefully to test several from it. Look for hooks that have a poor temper, have badly turned eyes, are too narrow in the gape, or have badly forged barbs (see Pic. 18, 19). Do not try to make one type of hook do the work of several — if you are worming use a long-shanked hook, then if you decide to change to maggots select a suitable, short-shanked hook. (34)

34   <u>Common hook faults</u>

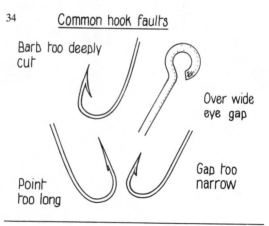

Barb too deeply cut

Over wide eye gap

Gap too narrow

Point too long

HOOK SIZES

As a general rule the size of the hook which will be selected is governed by the size of fish expected to be caught. The hook for a big 20 lb carp would hardly fit into the mouth of an 8 oz roach for instance. There are some exceptions to this rule, normally when small hooks have to be used for big fish. The tench is a good example — it has a relatively small and very soft mouth in comparison with its possible size and weight. (35)

35

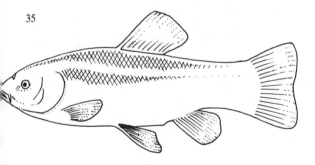

- Hooks are sized in numbers, on an even scale from 2 to 30, and the lower the number the larger the hook will be. A size 2 hook is around ¾ in long, a size 20 about ⅛ of an inch. Above size 2 the numbers have a suffix /0, and run in consecutive numbers — 1/0, 2/0, 3/0 and so on. (36)

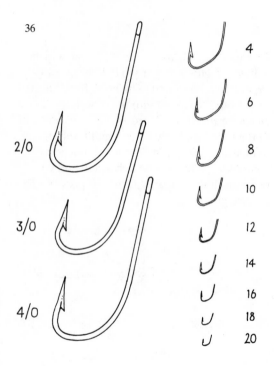

36

2/0

3/0

4/0

4

6

8

10

12

14

16

18

20

SHARPENING HOOKS

The best hook in the world will quickly blunt
in use. Just putting a bait on the hook can
cause it to lose its sharpness, and when the
hook is dragging the bottom it is suffering
constant wear. During and before fishing
hooks should be tested for sharpness against
the thumb-nail. (37)

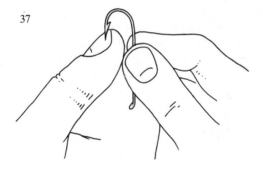

37

- To hone the point of a hook, use a
  sharpening stone purchased from the tackle
  shop. Make gentle strokes of the point along

the length of the stone and constantly check it as you do so. (38)

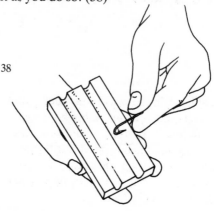

38

- The correct hook point is one that tapers gently, leaving a sharp-pointed, thin piece of metal for penetration. The wrong point has a short taper, leaving thick metal that will be difficult to drive home on the strike. (39)

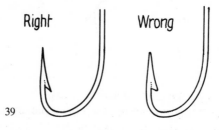

39

STORING HOOKS

Hooks left exposed to the damp will rust.
Hooks that are allowed to rattle around in
boxes of any sort will soon become blunt. Keep
your hooks folded in paper, stored in boxes. A
little thin oil will prevent them becoming rusty.
(40)

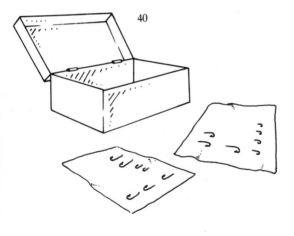

4 LINES AND KNOTS

INTRODUCTION

Although nylon was discovered back in the 1930s it only became available to anglers after the end of the Second World War. At that time it was spooled in lengths of high breaking strain, and did not have the smoothness and suppleness which we expect in today's product. Monofilament today is manufactured by a process called double-extrusion. The basic material is forced through nozzles of varying diameter and as it emerges it hardens. Under a carefully adjusted tension, the nylon then passes through infra-red radiation and as it does so its diameter hardens and takes on the required breaking strain (see Pic. 43).

Present-day lines are very versatile and possess strength, fineness, and a certain degree of resistance to kinking. But all monofilament tends to stretch when placed under strain. This of course is very much to the angler's advantage during a hard strike or when a fish makes a sudden sharp pull.

Unfortunately, there is a tendency for a degree of this stretch to remain in the line afterwards — and it is something that can continue to build up, weakening until eventually there is a considerable reduction in line circumference and its subsequent strength.

Yet another characteristic of monofilament is the fact that nylon has the ability to absorb between 3 and 13 per cent of its own weight of water. By this means the breaking strain of the line can be reduced by as much as 10 per cent.

Although nylon deteriorates slowly it must be remembered that long exposure to light can weaken it, especially in diameters of low breaking strains. So when you purchase line from the tackle shop, avoid selecting spools that appear to have been out on display for a long time. It is always better to ask for a fresh supply that has been kept in store.

Heat is another agent that helps to weaken monofilament and one over which the angler has little control. But bulk spools stored at home can and should be kept away from heat.

But now, having described the shortcomings of nylon monofilament, for all its faults it is a vast improvement on the materials the angler in the past had to use: horse-hair, strands of silkwork gut, cuttyhunk, jute, threads of all kinds — anything that a hook could be tied to without snapping at the first slight pull from a fish. Today's anglers should be grateful for that man-made substance we call nylon.

Finally, remember when you clean and oil your expensive reel that even a few drops of oil can cause damage to nylon. Separate the body of the reel from spool or drum and wipe surplus oil away immediately.

LINE STRENGTH

The strength of a nylon monofilament or braided line is measured in pounds or kilos of breaking strain. That is an indication of the strength of the line when it left the factory — but as we have seen, that need not mean the strength of line when it is used at the waterside. A number of factors can have affected its quality while in the shop or your tackle box.

Breaking strain at the factory is measured on special machines. A rather crude way for the angler at home to test the breaking strain of his line is to tie a length of it to a spring balance, and pull against that until the line breaks, noting the weight registered as it does so. But this is only a rough-and-ready guide and as we shall see later, every knot tied into a line weakens it.

Each time he puts his rod and reel together the prudent angler takes the end of the line from the reel and tests it by giving it a few stout tugs. If it has depreciated in strength then the line will snap easily and must immediately be discarded — not by being thrown away as it is,

but by cutting it up into short lengths, putting
it in a bag and sending it away with the
domestic refuse, or better still being burnt.
(41, 42)

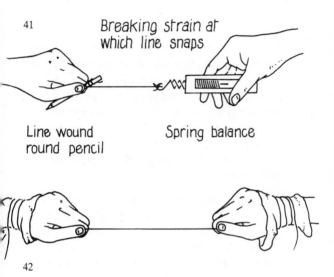

41

Breaking strain at
which line snaps

Line wound
round pencil

Spring balance

42

The quickest way to reduce the strength – and
therefore the breaking strain — of a line is to
repeatedly strain and stretch it — something
that is happening all the time in angling. Line
kink (constant twisting) is another strength-
reducing problem and should be guarded
against. Careful and thinking anglers renew all
their lines at very regular intervals; they know
that in the long run it is cheap.

SELECTING A LINE

The perfect line has yet to be invented. Most anglers use one line only to the exclusion of all others — even if they are unable to say why they like it. When choosing a line look for one that is pliable, though not given to over-stretching. Select one with as little glint as possible, something that if the sun catches it may put fish off from some distance, even underwater.

Many monofilament manufacturers advertise a low-glint quality with their natural-coloured lines. However, there is a great deal to be said for a coloured line either in blue, green or brown. A number of very experienced fishing enthusiasts are known to dye their lines in sections with a series of colours in an attempt to avoid glint altogether and at the same time merge it into coloured water.

BRAIDED LINES

Lines that are braided from nylon or dacron are softer than monofilament, less prone to lose strength when wet and knot easily. But they do not last long, cling when leaving the drum of a reel and also create more friction when running over the spool lip of a fixed spool reel. (43)

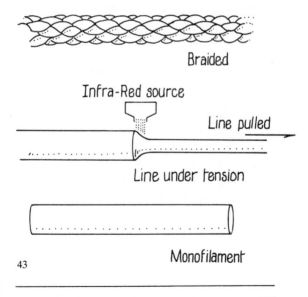

Braided

Infra-Red source

Line pulled

Line under tension

Monofilament

43

- Additionally, they are more easily seen by fish in the water because of their considerably thicker diameter, much thicker than monofilament. Their qualities make them excellent for sea fishing or trolling, but not for general use by the freshwater angler, who needs fine and sometimes very fine line which does not advertise its presence in clear, fresh shallow water inhabited by extremely wary fish.

LOADING LINE

Always load your line on to the reel so that it avoids imparting a twist or kink. In the case of centrepin and multiplying reels line can be run on in a straight, direct way (44) off the

44

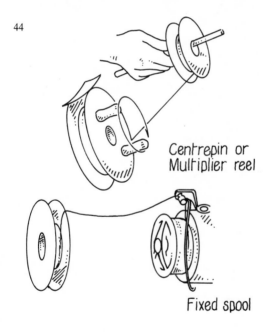

Centrepin or
Multiplier reel

Fixed spool

manufacturer's spool, using a little tension to prevent the line coils bunching. Fixed-spool reels should be loaded with the line spool held at an angle of about 90 degrees, allowing the line to pull over its rim. By loading line in this fashion the bale arm will wind on without twisting the line. (44)

KNOTS

It has to be accepted that every knot that is tied in nylon monofilament will weaken the strength of the line. The amount of strength that is lost will depend on which knot has been used because some are less damaging than others. The biggest problem comes with strangulation — the knot pulls tighter and tighter until it literally cuts the line in half. The following knots have been selected because they have been proved as being kind to line. They are shown in a series of step-by-step illustrations to allow you to practise tying them at home rather than at the waterside. Anyone who has tried to tie an unfamiliar knot in thin nylon, with cold, wet hands, will know what the problem is.

The Blood Knot

A universal knot where nylon line is concerned. This knot is the means whereby two ends of monofilament can be joined without their slipping apart, attaching a hook line to the reel line, or joining line to backing.

- Start by laying both ends to be joined beside each other. (45)

45

- Twist one free end four times round the body of the other and tuck it between the two parts. (46)

46

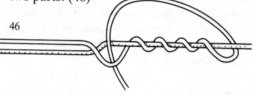

- Repeat with the other end. (47)

47

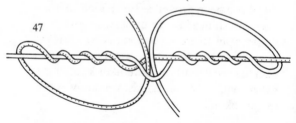

- Draw the knot tight, remembering to moisten it before giving the final pull. This will allow it to slide easily into place without strangling. (48)

48

Tucked Half Blood Knot

This knot is used where a swivel or eyed hook
needs to be attached to the line.

■ Pass the end of the line through the eye.
(49)

49

■ Twist the end round the standing part four
or five times. (50)

50

■ Pass the end through the main loop (51)
and —

51

■ Once again through the larger loop before
moistening, and pulling tight. (52)

52

Blood Loop Dropper Knot

Here is a knot for making a paternoster loop or a dropper in a fly cast.

■ Make a circle with long overlapping ends and keep twisting the end around the original circle, making some 10 smaller ones. (53)

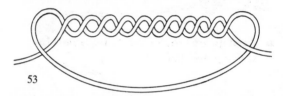

53

■ Enlarge the centre loop and push the original circle back through it. (54)

54

■ Moisten, then pull the ends tight holding a finger in the loop to prevent it sliding closed. (55)

55

Double Loop Knot

Any time a loop is needed in the end of a line, use the double loop non-slip knot.

■ Form a bend in the end of the line. (56)

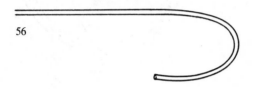

56

■ Make an overhand knot from it. (57)

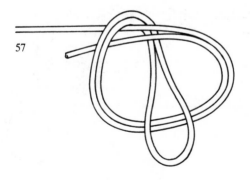

57

■ Then make two or three more turns (58) before —

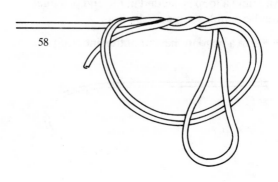

58

■ moistening and pulling the knot tight. (59)

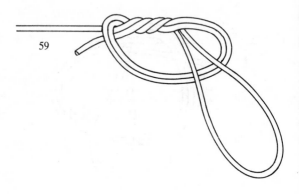

59

Blood Bight

Another simple knot that will form a loop
quickly — even in the dark.

■ Form a loop in the end of the line. (60)

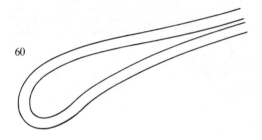

60

■ Wrap the end of the loop several times
around the body. (61)

61

■ Pass the loop end back through its last turn. (62)

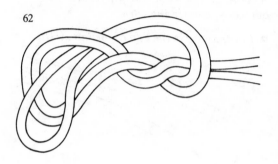

62

■ Moisten, then pull tight. (63)

63

Dipped Loops

An easy and quick method of putting tackle together, especially hooks ready tied to nylon.

- Tie two double loop knots (see Pic. 56-59) in the end of the line, leaving the loops long.

- Pass one loop through the other and —

- Pass the hook end through the line loop

- Pull gently together. (64)

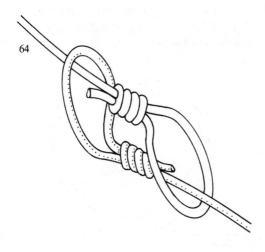

64

Water Knot

With a high breaking strain, the knot is useful for tying a leader with several droppers.

■ Hold the ends so that there is enough overlap. (65)

65

■ Form a loop and pull the right-hand end through the loop from behind making an overhand knot. (66)

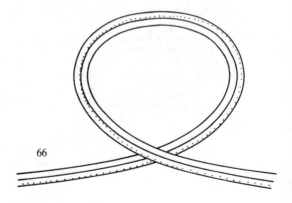

66

- Repeat four times (67) and then —

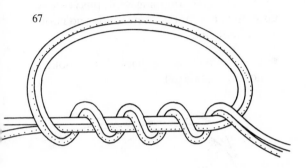

67

- Moisten before pulling tight. The fly should be fastened to the end of line which runs towards the rod, on which the fly will stand out. (68)

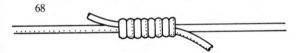

68

Spade End Knot

Often called the whipping knot, this is the universal knot for attaching spade end hooks to the hook line.

■ Lay a loop along the shank of the hook, holding both. (69)

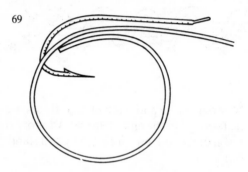

69

■ Make a turn round the shank over the end of the hook. (70)

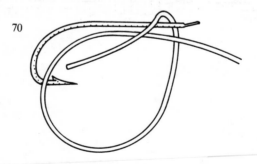

70

- Make another turn passing over the first. (71)

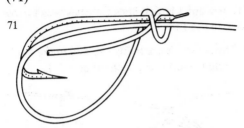

71

- Take five turns more along the shank. (72)

72

- Pass the line end through the loop and pull tight. (73)

73

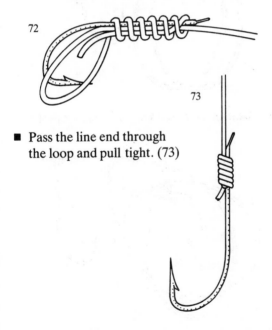

Two-Circle Turle Knot

This is a quickly tied knot for attaching an eyed hook to the line.

- Thread the hook by its eye and make two circles, overlaying each other. (74)

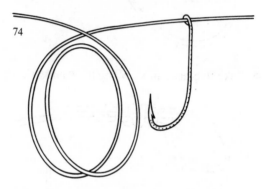

- Make an overhand knot over the loops. (75)

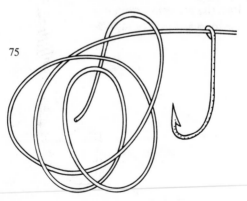

■ Tighten and ease the hook through the circles. (76)

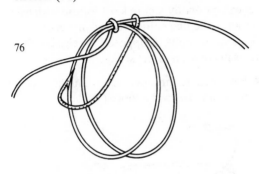

76

■ Pull tight. (77)

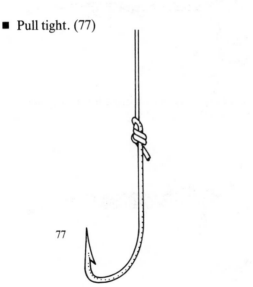

77

Domhof Knot

An exceptionally secure knot for use with eyed hooks — the line being secured around the shank of the hook as opposed to the eye. This helps make for a direct strike.

- Pass the line through the eye and lay it along the shank to form a loop. (78)

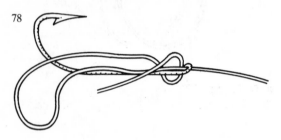

- Take eight turns round the loop and pass the end through. (79)

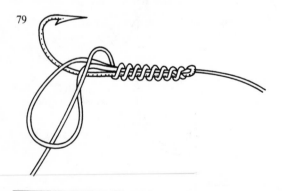

■ Moisten and pull tight. (80)

80

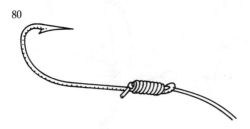

Buckle Swivel Loop

An easy means of attaching a buckle swivel to the line and releasing it equally quickly.

■ Make a loop in the end of the line. (81)

81

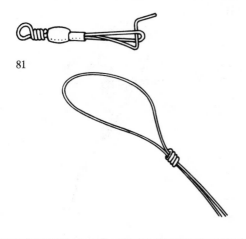

- Pass the loop through the eye of the swivel. (82)

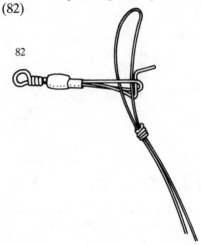

82

- Put the loop over the wire end of the swivel. (83)

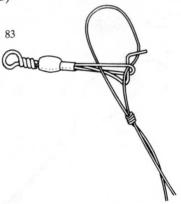

83

■ Clear it. (84)

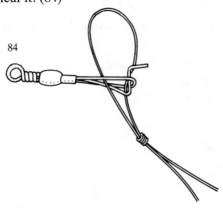

84

■ And let it ease into place. (85)

85

Barrel, or Stop Knot

An adjustable knot for use with a sliding float.
The knot will wind onto the line easily.

■ Take 6 in of line similar to that being used
and loop it along the line where the stop is
required. (86)

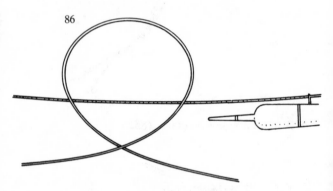

86

■ Pass one end over the reel line five or six
times. (87)

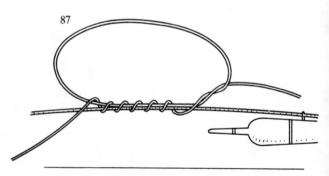

87

■ Hold the reel line firm and pull both ends of the loop to form a solid knot. (88)

■ Cut the ends free. (89)

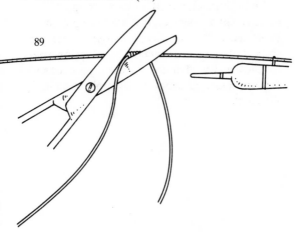

■ The finished knot. (90)

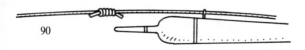

The knots described above will take an angler through his fishing career. There is one salient test for a knot in nylon: its tying must not affect the line's breaking strain, for a badly tied knot will exert sufficient pressure on itself to snap the weakest part. There are many knots of great assistance to those anglers who carry out their fishing from boats. The half-hitch, clove hitch, bowline, reef, sheet bend, all have their value when afloat. One novel sea angler's knot is the Policanski, which forms a strong attachment to a swivel. But knot tying is an exact art, perhaps a science. Anglers interested should read the knot sections in encyclopedias, for they may well discover a use for a knot so far unrecognised as having an application in the sport.

5 SWIVELS, LINKS AND WEIGHTS

INTRODUCTION

For those anglers who spin or who use live or deadbaits for pike and perch fishing, the swivel is an essential piece of angling equipment. It is almost impossible to eliminate line kink altogether, because every time a hard-fighting fish is played some twist and kink is caused to the line, but swivels can reduce the nuisance drastically, something that will keep the breaking strain of the line high and prolong its life.

Swivels and links are small items of tackle that cost mere pence, but they are probably the most abused and misunderstood aids in the myriad of angling's fishing accessories. For many anglers their presence is regarded as essential and any old swivel — the first that comes to hand — is fitted somewhere along the line. In fact there are a number of different swivels and links on the market and using the wrong one can be more counter-productive than using none at all.

In exactly the same way as hooks, swivels are sized and numbered, the smallest being size

18, the largest 8/0, designed for heavy sea fishing, are immensely strong. Like hooks, the more you pay then the higher the quality and, more important still, the better they will revolve. Good swivels are bronzed — the best are manufactured from stainless steel. Some have ball-bearings incorporated in the housing and there are a number of brass swivels on the market but these are intended for sea fishing and tend to wear quite quickly.

Box Swivels

■ Box swivels are among the earliest form of swivel and they are still manufactured and readily available from tackle shops. Though they were designed for sea fishing they are available in smaller sizes suitable for coarse fishing. In terms of efficiency they are poor performers, the pull through the swivel jamming the moving parts against the body of the swivel itself. Box swivels are also capable of picking up grit and weed in the exposed moving parts — although, on the plus side, this can be seen and removed. They are better left alone by the freshwater angler because for his special purposes there are better kinds. (91)

91

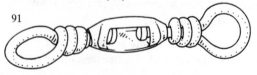

Barrel Swivels

- These are by far the most common swivel
  for freshwater fishing. They are available in
  blued steel and are long lasting.
  Unfortunately, by virtue of their
  construction, they allow grit and dirt to
  enter into the concealed body and after a
  little use fail to turn at all. They should be
  constantly checked while in use. (92)

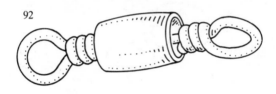

92

Ball Bearing Swivels

- The best of all swivels — but because they
  are the best they are the most expensive. A
  high quality metal body incorporates ball
  bearings that ensure the swivel will not jam
  regardless of the pressure and pull that is
  applied to it. (93)

93

Three-Way Swivels

■ These are designed for use with the
paternoster rig, where special three-way
swivels eliminate a great deal of line twist
not just to the reel line, but to the trace as
well. The smaller sizes are expensive but
well worth the initial outlay. (94)

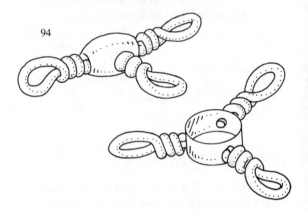

94

LINK SWIVELS

Link swivels are designed to allow quick attachment and release of the line, at the same time helping eliminate line kink. There are several models on the market with different methods of attachment and it is worth remembering that the simplest is the best. This especially applies when the angler is fishing on a bitterly cold day, and is trying to change a lure or hook link with frozen fingers.

Link Swivel

- The link is operated by being compressed between finger and thumb, allowing the loop of a hook link or lure to be slid into the swivel centre. These swivels are useful in large sizes — but unless the metal is of good quality, link swivels are likely to pull straight in the smaller ranges. (95)

95

Spring Link Swivel

- One of the most commonly used of all
  swivels. The sprung half circles at the link
  end are prised open and line or lure passed
  between and into the link's centre. These
  are not the best of swivels — there is a
  tendency for the half circles to open during
  use, loosening the attachment that is being
  used. They are also difficult to manipulate
  during cold weather when fingers are wet
  and clumsy. (96)

2 kinds of
Spring Link swivel

96

Buckle Link Swivel

- Principally an item from the sea angler's
  tackle box, the buckle link is simple to use
  and rarely becomes prised open. It is
  unfortunate that buckle link swivels are

only available in large sizes, so the
freshwater angler misses out. (97)

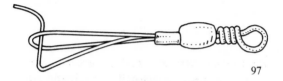

97

Snap Link Swivels

- Universally used and provided they are
  manufactured from good-quality metal, and
  with the clip end well-tempered, snap link
  swivels are highly efficient. When using
  snap link swivels, watch that a build up of
  trapped weed at the snap end doesn't gag
  the locking pieces open. (98)

Snap Link swivel

Snap Link Diamond Eye

98

CARE OF SWIVELS

During the course of just a few days fishing all swivels can become jammed with grit and dried weed which forces its way into the body and stops that all-important anti-kink action. This happens to a lesser degree with the ball bearing swivel too, but even these require some servicing if they are to give of their best.

- Before the fishing season opens, check all swivels at home and look for signs of wear at the loop end — friction from nylon line can cut into soft metal with ease.

- Drop these swivels into an egg cup and add some Swarfega or other recommended degreasant to help clean out trapped dirt.

- Wash the swivels well in water, and dry them thoroughly — a little heat will help evaporate moisture.

- Oil with a little WD 40 or similar light oil.

ANTI-KINK DEVICES

These are designed to help the anti-kink action of swivels, the best kinds attaching to the body of the swivel itself to prevent it from revolving.

K'neverkink

- The simplest anti-kink device, now well established and a great favourite, this torpedo-shaped plastic tube slips onto the line and is then pushed down onto the swivel itself. Not 100 per cent efficient, but is easy to mount and cheap enough to lose without too much financial embarrassment. (99)

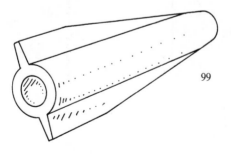

99

Plastic Vane and Swivel

■ This is another simple device. Hanging
  down from the body of the swivel, the vane
  prevents the body twisting and makes it
  work efficiently. It is not cheap, and is
  prone to snapping free when a lure is
  retrieved through heavy weed. Problems
  can be overcome by giving them occasional
  checks. (100)

Clear plastic vane
with ball bearing swivel

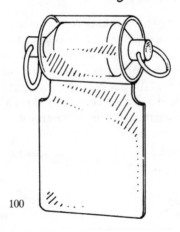

100

Swivel with Celluloid Vane

- Here is probably the most certain method of preventing line kink. The vane end is tied to the reel link, the swivel receiving the hook link or trace. If there is any disadvantage in this device it is that fish will occasionally be tempted to strike at the vane and not at the hook-bearing lure behind it. (101)

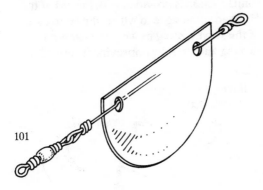

101

WEIGHTS

The use of lead weights to prevent line turning is the principle of the half-moon lead which clips onto the reel line above the swivels. A similar action is provided with the aid of the Hillman spinning lead which clips into one eye of the swivel, using its weight to stop it from turning and thereby improving its efficiency.

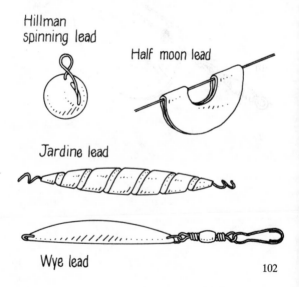

Hillman
spinning lead

Half moon lead

Jardine lead

Wye lead

102

The Wye lead with a link swivel is slightly boat-shaped and this stops the line from turning, causing the swivel to revolve. (102)

All of these devices possess a serious disadvantage in that they will make the bait 'keyhole'. Being heavy, there is a tendency for the weight to lead the bait when the cast is made, causing the two elements of the tackle to tangle together during flight. This can be avoided by reducing the weight of lead used — but the result is usually a reduction in the efficiency of the anti-kinking action. (103)

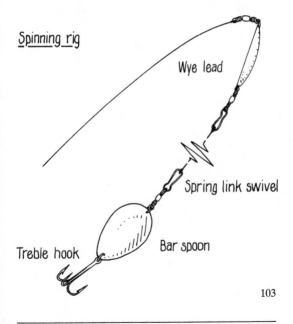

Spinning rig

Wye lead

Spring link swivel

Treble hook   Bar spoon

103

PART III
BAITS

Angling receives a constant flow of newcomers to the sport who must at their introduction face a bewildering complex not only of the 'tools of the trade', the rods, reels, hooks, accessories, styles and so on, but the apparently endless list of baits constantly discussed in the columns of angling books and journals.

But the novice need not stagger back, eyes popping and aghast at the array of tackle and baits on display in tackle shops, because this book has been planned to present the newcomer to coarse fishing with an easy introduction to angling's basic needs.

This section, concerned with angler's coarse-fishing baits, describes and illustrates the majority of offerings that the newcomer to the sport might consider. There are others, of course, as well as many contributions of those described, but as the thinking angler gains more and more experience there will come a desir to take these standard baits and experiment with others.

6 TYPES OF BAIT

INTRODUCTION

The angler's fishing baits are items of food that will entice a fish into feeding so that bait and the hook on which it is impaled will finish up in its mouth. No matter how expensive and sensible an angler's outfit of fishing tackle may be and how expertly he fishes it will all be wasted unless the bait that is used actually attracts fish. To do that a bait must be one of several things.

First it must be fresh. Rarely will fish be attracted to something that is offensive, smells, or tastes rotten. This especially applies to natural baits such as worms, deadbaits, freshwater mussels, and so on. This means that great care should be taken when baits are gathered and prepared, when and how they are kept, and during the time that they are carried to the waterside. More anglers fail to catch fish through baits that are bad and unacceptable to fish than through any other possible cause. This is borne out by L-anglers, fishing clumsily and probably breaking all the rules about care, quiet, stealth and so on, and yet catching fish because they happened to have just the right bait at the right place, at the right time.

Secondly, baits must be attractive – and that means visually as well as gastronomically. Remember that once the bait is in the water it has to be seen or smelled by the fish, often when the water is coloured or when the swim being fished is deep and correspondingly dark. It is therefore obvious that without the all-important element of attractiveness in his bait the angler might just as well fish with a bare hook.

There are, of course, other ways of tempting fish other than by using baits. Spinners, plugs, lures of every colour, shape and size, are splendid fish-takers. But this small volume must concentrate on the angler's hook-baits alone, leaving the huge subject of lures for a possible later volume in this series.

Groundbaits are used by the angler to bring fish into the area in which his hookbait is waiting. Like hookbaits, groundbaits must be fresh and attractive – but not of such wholesome quality that the hookbait itself is ignored. Where this is possible, the bait on the hook must always be just that little bit more obvious. As an example, one whole herring used as a legered hookbait stands out among chopped-up pieces of herring thrown loosely around it.

Although groundbaits are normally used in fairly large quantities they still need to be carefully prepared and properly transported to the waterside if they are to be in tip-top condition on the day that they are used. This means that the angler must take his time and carefully plan the assembly of all the materials he will need well in advance.

PREPARING BAITS

Many baits which the angler uses require
cooking, especially those of the pasta and seed
kinds. It is as well to have your own saucepans
for these, and to make sure that you have a
strainer to drain unwanted fluid away after
boiling. One of the fine-mesh metal types is
ideal, capable of dealing with ingredients up to
a pound in weight.

Deadbaits can be purchased and stored in
advance. Make sure that you have plenty of
plastic bags, and that there is room in the
freezer for them. It is also better to label each
bag with the contents and date of freezing, so
keep a supply of freezer labels that are
designed to stick despite the cold.

Many natural baits must be kept alive before
use, and some are better when bred by the
angler – slugs are an example. A very large
aquarium is a sensible investment, to be kept
in a dark corner, perhaps in the garage. Feed
the slugs on lettuce leaves, potato-peelings
and so on, and cover with a lid with air-holes
to keep them from straying. Even during the
depths of winter the 'slug store' will provide

good baits and so prove its worth when collecting outside is virtually impossible.

Pike anglers who are committed to livebaiting will obviously think of building a pond in which to keep baits, so avoiding the problem of catching them during the winter months. A better consideration is a large tank, such as a galvanised cattle drinking-trough, plumbed to allow a supply of water to circulate. It can be kept in an outhouse or garage.

KEEPING BAITS

Cereal and seed-type baits are best chilled
after preparation and should be kept in the
fridge. Light and transparent Tuppaware or
similar airtight and watertight containers are
ideal for this purpose. Maggots are best kept
chilled after purchase, and again plastic boxes
are ideal. Some natural baits from the
waterside such as swan mussels or caddis
larvae, must be kept in an aquarium until the
angler leaves home. Then they need to be
carried and kept wet in fresh, damp weed, not
water. This kind of bait must not be confined
in a small space, so they sometimes require
larger-than-usual watertight boxes.

CARRYING BAITS

Hook baits are normally carried in plastic boxes, perforated with air holes in the case of maggots or worms both of which require oxygen. Make sure that the boxes you buy are the right shape and size to fit into your bag or box seat. It is better to standardise them than to have a non-matching collection that requires fitting in your tackle-box like a jigsaw puzzle.

Livebaits are best carried in a large plastic box fitted with a close-fitted lid and handle. Those used to carry plaster and other products of the building industry are ideal – a visit to a building site can sometimes pay dividends. They are expensive, but battery-driven aerators are a must if baits are to be kept alive on any but the shortest of journeys.

Groundbaits are usually carried dry to the waterside and then mixed there so that they adopt the taint of the local water. A sizable canvas bucket is perfect for this task both to carry to the waterside and to mix the groundbait in. Always have expendable pieces of towel to wipe your hands on after mixing groundbait and handling hookbaits.

CEREAL BAITS

Bread

- This is an all-round bait that will attract many different species of fish. It is usually used with a light, powdery groundbait. One large loaf will provide sufficient bait for the average day's sport. (1)

1

Floating crust

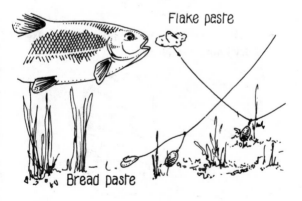

Flake paste

Bread paste

Bread Paste

- Remove the soft inside of a loaf at the waterside. (2)

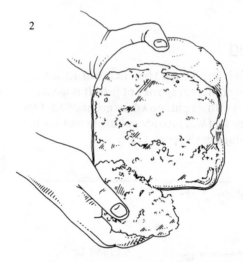

- Dip it once into the water and then squeeze it dry immediately. (3).

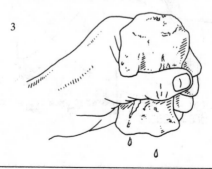

- Mould it in a piece of clean, damp rag until it is stiff, and then keep it dry during the day. Pieces can be pulled free and moulded around the hook as required. (4)

4

- Processed cheese, luncheon meat, sausage meat – all these soft products are very attractive to fish and can be moulded into the bait as the paste is made. It is a good way of presenting them. (5, 6)

5

6

■ Bread paste can be coloured red, pink, or
  yellow by adding blancmange powder once
  it has been made damp. Colours often
  attract fish when the plain bait fails. (7)

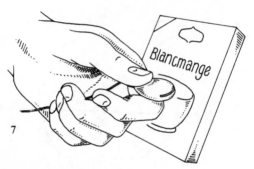

Bread Flake

■ Bread flake is made by pulling a piece of
  soft inside from a loaf and moulding it round
  the shank of the hook, leaving the bend and
  point exposed. (8, 9)

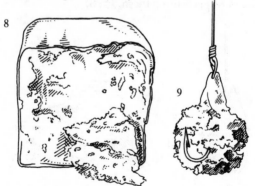

■ Naturally, a fresh loaf is best. When not required the loaf should be kept wrapped in a damp cloth to keep it from drying out and going stale.

Floating Crust

■ This is a favourite bait for surface-feeding fish such as rudd, chub and carp. It is formed by tearing a piece of crust from a loaf, leaving some soft underside beneath the brown outer surface. Some anglers cut it to form a cube rather than tear an irregular-shaped piece to be mounted on the hook. The shape is of no consequence to the fish. It is important that the crust is soft and not hard, otherwise the hook will break free during the cast. (10)

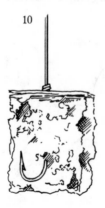

Crust

- Crust is a sinking type of bait that takes time to prepare but which is an old and tested fish-catcher. Start by taking the base and sides from a square loaf of bread. (11)

11

- Wrap it in a damp cloth. (12)

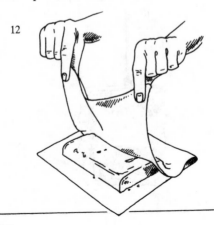

12

■ Place it between two off-cuts of wood. (13)

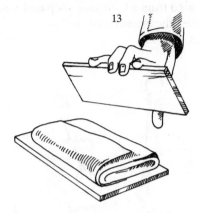

■ Now put weight on the boards to compress the crust between them – the leg of a table often comes in handy! (14)

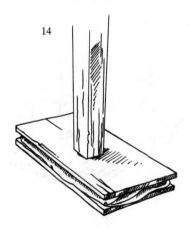

- Better are two cheap cramps which can be purchased from a hardware shop and which will press the bread tightly between the boards. (15, 16)

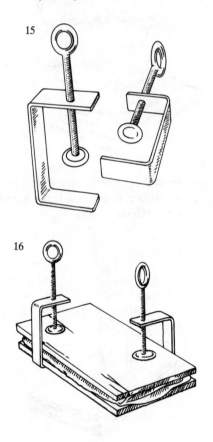

15

16

■ Leave overnight and the next day remove
the bread and cut the crust into strips, then
into small cubes or triangles, which will
move well in the water. Store in a plastic
box. (17)

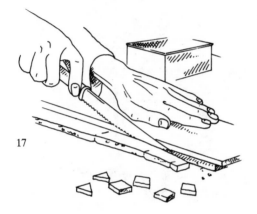

17

Punched Bread

■ A bread punch makes small, hard pellets of
soft bread quickly and efficiently. The
punch can be purchased at a tackle dealers
and usually comes with several head sizes.
(18)

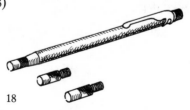

18

■ A slice of white bread is put onto a hard
surface and the bread punch is pushed hard
onto it. (19)

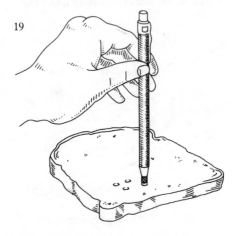

19

■ Bait the hook from bread in the punch –
don't try to pull the bread free and then put
it on the hook.

■ Once the hook is into the bread slide it
carefully from the punch. An excellent bait
for roach fishing, when this species is
proving finicky.

Flour Paste

■ Another soft hook-bait easily made at home
before setting out. Spoon plain flour into a
bowl. (20)

20

■ Add water and mix until there is a stiff
dough and then turn it into a damp rag, or
store it in a small plastic box to keep and
carry. (21)

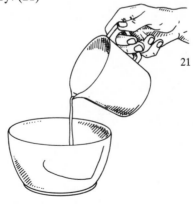

21

- Colour and sweetness often add to
  attraction – use sugar, blancmange powder
  or custard powder for the best results. (22)

22

SEED AND PASTA-TYPE BAITS

Often considered old-fashioned by modern anglers, these are tried and tested favourites that can sometimes be a problem to mount onto a hook. But with perseverance and common sense they can produce results when many other baits fail. (23)

23

Wheat and Pearl Barley

- Both of these are all-the-year-round baits, with pearl barley often being used as a groundbait to the larger wheat grains. Wheat, also known as creed, used to be more popular than it is today. Prepare them separately – a pound of either is sufficient for a day's fishing. (24)

24

Pearl Barley

Wheat

■ Cover the grains with water or milk in a saucepan and then stew them until the white kernel of the grain is just, and *only just* showing. (25)

25

- Avoid over-cooking at all costs – this can make the seed impossible to mount onto a hook. Use a sieve to wash the grains under a cold tap when it is ready, and cold-store in the fridge with a plastic box, taking care to keep the grains moist. Especially in warm weather, keep refrigerated until you are ready to leave home. (26)

26

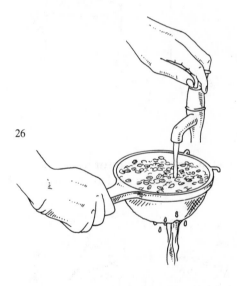

- Another, easier way to cook wheat and pearl barley is to half-fill a vacuum flask with the grains, filling the remainder of the flask with boiling water. Left overnight, the bait will be ready cooked in the morning –

but remember to cool it once the flask is opened, otherwise the cooking action will continue. (27)

27

Rice

■ Both types of rice, short (or round) and long grained, can be used by the angler. (28)

28

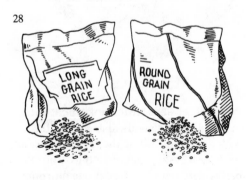

■ Long-grained rice is easier to use on the
hook, short grained makes groundbait.
Tiny though this bait is, it produces
excellent results with roach and dace,
especially with ultra-fine tackle. Prepare in
exactly the same way as wheat and pearl
barley but wash in the sieve with hot, not
cold water. This will prevent it from
lumping. (29)

29

Hempseed

■ Good quality hempseed is a winning bait,
especially for the match angler. It needs
careful preparation if it is to stay on the

hook. A pound is normally sufficient for a day. (30)

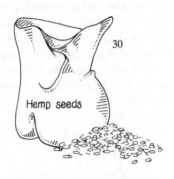

- Cover the seed with water in a saucepan and bring to the boil. (31)

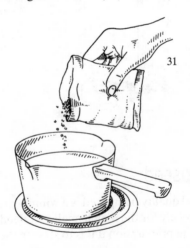

- Add a teaspoon full of sugar and soda to give sweetness and to intensify the blackness of the seed. (32, 33)

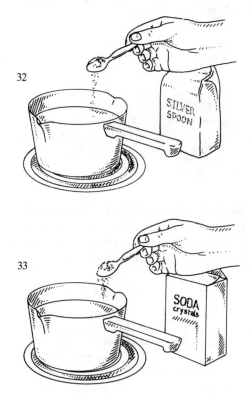

- Simmer until the white kernel of the seed shows – as for cooking wheat.

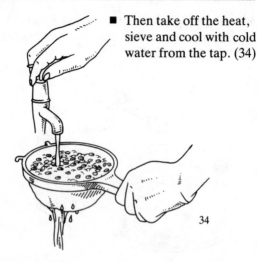

■ Then take off the heat, sieve and cool with cold water from the tap. (34)

34

■ Store the grains, still damp, in an airtight box in the fridge until required. Once at the waterside, dampen the grains again – dried seeds will float and not sink. (35)

35

Sweetcorn

- An expensive but universal bait. It can be used frozen, lightly cooked or straight out of a can. It quickly dries out and should be kept out of direct sunlight on the bank. (36)

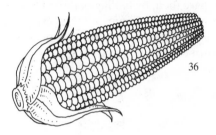

36

- The seeds need to be broadcast over a wide area – a catapult is virtually a necessity for this purpose. One or two seeds on the hook are normal, more if you are legering. (37)

37

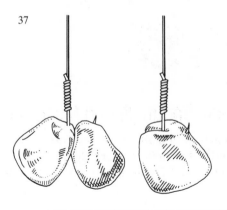

Tares

■ These big seeds – more than twice the size
  of hempseed – are ideal for use as a
  hookbait. They are very visible to the fish
  and are easily mounted on the hook.
  Prepare them by boiling in the same way as
  for hemp. Both hemp and tares can also be
  cooked using the thermos-flask principle
  shown for wheat preparation. (38)

38

Pasta, Spaghetti and Macaroni

■ Small pasta shells of various sizes will spin
  and turn with the current. Spaghetti and
  macaroni will wriggle and turn, worm-like,

in the water. All these actions are attractive to fish. (39)

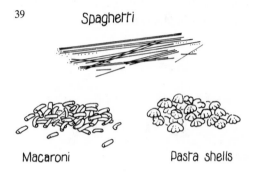

Macaroni   Pasta shells

■ All of these baits should be gently cooked in milk or water until they are soft, then drained and stored in airtight boxes in the fridge until required. (40)

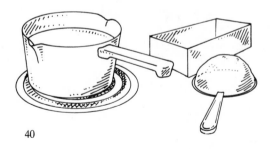

■ Both spaghetti and macaroni should be cut
into small pieces before being mounted
onto the hook. They are best threaded onto
the line first, the hook being tied on after
the bait is in place. (41)

41

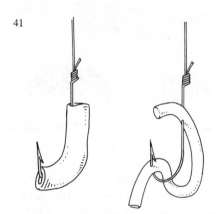

VEGETABLE BAITS

Though alien to fish in their natural surroundings these baits are often taken by fish, especially by bottom-feeding species, though they may take some time to become educated into accepting them.

Potato

- Universally accepted as a carp bait, the potato can be offered in slices, moulded from instant mix into balls, or whole, when it is par-boiled. (42)

42

■ Select potatoes in the marble- to golf-ball
   sizes for par-boiling. New potatoes are
   especially useful for this. Leave their skins
   on while cooking takes place, after which
   they can be scraped using a pan scrub to get
   smoothness. Boil them long enough to
   become soft. When they dent under
   pressure from finger and thumb they are
   done. Tinned potatoes are ready made for
   the job – but expensive. (43)

43

■ Potatoes, or pieces of them are mounted
  whole on to the hook. Use a baiting needle
  to pull line through and then tie the hook
  on behind it. Make sure that the point
  protrudes. (44)

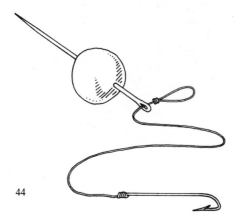

44

Peas

■ An easy bait to mount on the hook, peas
  can be frozen, dried or tinned. Various
  dried varieties reconstituted and boiled,
  using the producer's instructions, make an
  excellent groundbait, especially if over-
  cooked to the point of being mushy, when
  they produce an attractive carpet on the

bottom. Frozen or tinned peas are best for the hook. Remember to keep them moist throughout the day. (45)

45

FRUIT BAITS

While many baits we use are completely new
to fish, it is possible that they may see at least a
few of these. In their natural state fruits are
summer specials, but one or two are worth
collecting and freezing for use at other times,
in combination with other baits.

Blackberries

- A well-proven chub bait where bushes
  overhang the water. Choose well-ripened
  fruit, freshly gathered. Free-cast a few
  berries before offering the fish the berry in
  which the hook is concealed.
  The variety known as dew
  berries, where each fruit
  segment is twice the
  normal size, is extra-
  soft and juicy and well
  worth the trouble of
  looking for as the
  hook bait. (46)

46

Elderberries and Blackcurrants

- Both elderberries and blackcurrants are
  useful baits on their own. But their main
  attraction comes when combined with
  hempseed. The extra size over that of a
  single hemp grain mounted on to a hook,
  the ease with which it is mounted and the
  jet-black appearance will bring a more
  steady, determined bite from fish that often
  snatch at free-falling grains. Both berries
  are worth gathering in season and
  preserving or freezing for use during the
  winter. (47)

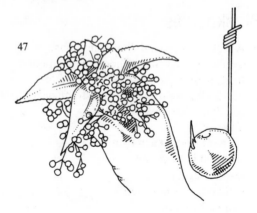

47

Cherries

■ Cherries are another bait associated with
chub, but which have accounted for both
tench and carp. They were first used as a
seasonal bait at Thames weirs, freelined
into the water beside the lasher. Fresh
cherries must be carefully stoned and then
mounted onto a very fine treble hook, the
edges being folded over and pushed through
the soft fruit until the points of the hook
show. Cocktail cherries and cherries used in
confectionery cooking are excellent, besides
being ready for mounting onto a hook. But
it is cheaper to use the natural fruit as free-
offered groundbait. (48)

48

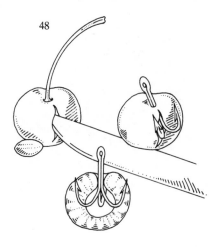

Banana

■ Another of the off-beat baits that sometimes
turns up trumps. Worked into bread paste,
with honey or treacle added, the result can
be irresistible to carp. Its softness, however,
makes banana difficult to cast on its own,
and even when combined with a stiffening
medium it still comes away easily from the
hook. Small cubes can be used when long-
trotting, providing that no long-distance
casting has to be undertaken. (49)

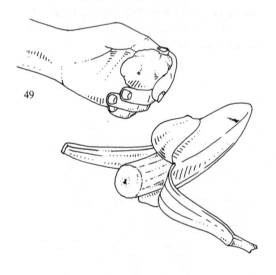

49

CHEESE

Appearance, flavour and ease of presentation make this an all-round bait that has accounted for fish of every variety – even sizable pike. Too much emphasis cannot be laid on the fact that any kind of cheese selected and used must be fresh. (50)

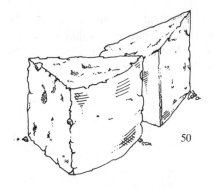

50

■ Hard cheeses can be cut into cubes, triangles or oblongs (the shape encourages movement in the current) and these can be mounted onto the hook making sure that the point of the hook always shows through.

Vary the size of the shapes – cheese cubes tend to float slightly and bigger pieces can help long-trotting tactics. (51)

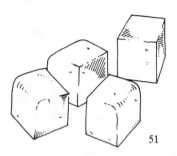

51

■ Soft cheeses can be mounted onto the hook and processed cheeses, sealed in foil, are ideal for this style, moisture being retained while they remain packed. (52)

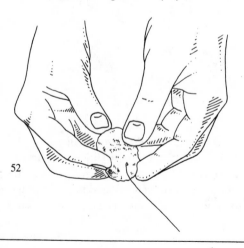

52

- Hard cheeses can be moulded after being grated with a kitchen grater and then added to bread paste. This method is especially useful when some of the more 'smelly' varieties of cheeses such as Danish Blue and Stilton are being considered. (53)

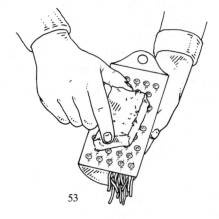

53

MEAT BAITS

These are baits full of surprises. Barbel, carp,
bream – all at some time will feed voraciously
on the various meat baits offered to them by
anglers. Presentation is everything when using
solid meat, and you must be prepared to fiddle
with a baiting needle if your bait is going to be
kept on the hook during casting.

Luncheon Meat

- There are a number of varieties of luncheon
  meat, some going under trade names.
  Basically all are compressed and processed
  meat in tins that are easily carried and can
  be opened on the bank. (54)

54

- Remember to have a tin-opener in your tackle-box in case the built-in one breaks. Heat will make the meat soft and greasy, so retain the tins in a fridge overnight and keep them cool during the day. The cooler the bait is kept, the easier it is to cut into cubes.

- It is worth the trouble of carrying a cutting board and sharp knife with which to cut the meat baits. Cubes are easiest, and once cut, put the pieces back into the tin to help keep them grease-free and solid. (55)

55

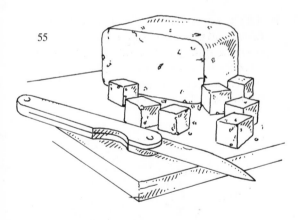

- Use a baiting needle to pass the line through the bait, pulling the hook up against the meat. Take care not to pull the hook too tightly into the cube otherwise you will pad the point and possibly prevent it driving home. (56)

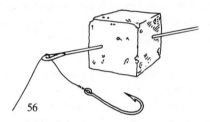

56

Corned beef

■ Again, a meat bait that lends itself to being cubed and threaded onto the hook. But its coarse texture means that it doesn't remain attached for long once it is under water. Better to crumble it and then work it into a base of bread paste. (57)

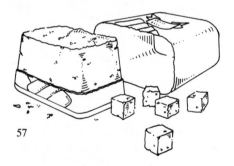

57

Sausage

■ Sausage meat, as opposed to sausages, makes an excellent additive to paste for the hook. It also works easily into a solid kind of groundbait. Some anglers have had success by working the meat into cubes or balls, then lightly frying them. The treatment serves to keep the bait on the hook. (58)

58

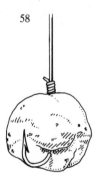

Bacon Fat and Rind

■ Like all meat baits, bacon is unpredictable so far as results are concerned. Strips of fat and short lengths of rind, hooked at one end and long-trotted with a float, will work, worm-like, in the water and can be very effective. The bait is largely and successfully used in the US; one of the ways in which it is presented by American anglers is by being attached to the treble hook on a spinner or plug and allowed to trail behind the lure during a retrieve. (59)

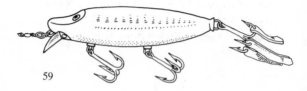

59

HIGH-PROTEIN BAITS

Better purchased in powder form from your tackle shop, high-protein (or HP) baits contain casein (milk protein) and the vitamin B complex found in yeast. These are soluble in water. (60)

Recipe for a DIY high protein bait

CASILAN — 1oz

mix with beaten eggs (10oz dry mix to 6 standard eggs)

GLUTEN — 1oz

LACTALBUMIN — 1oz

EQUIVITE — 1oz

SOYA FLOUR — 1oz

CASEIN — 5oz

■ HP baits can be prepared at home, starting
with half a dozen eggs added to a mixture of
wheatgerm, soya flour, yeast and casein.
Mix the eggs and powder (home-prepared
or shop bought) into a paste. Break into
small balls and then boil these for a minute
or so, until the outer skin toughens. It is
possible to add smell to the bait by mixing
in gravy powder, Marmite and so on, during
the preparation. The whole concept of using
HP baits is open to experiment and
imagination. (61, 62)

61

62

- Another method of HP presentation is to mix the ingredients together and then to deep-freeze them uncooked. Carried to the waterside in a vacuum flask, the frozen baits can easily be added to the hook and cast out. But once in the water the bait will melt, becoming soft and allowing its flavour to spread into the surrounding water.

NATURAL BAITS

Free for the taking, and completely acceptable to every species of fish, predators and browsers, natural baits should be high on the angler's menu card. But you need to know when and where to search for them, as well as how they are best kept, if you are going to be sure of an adequate and continual supply. (63)

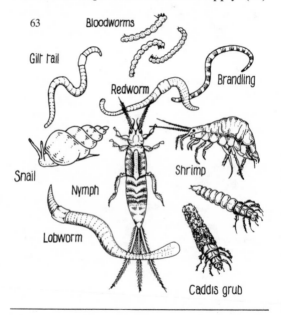

63

Bloodworms

Gilt tail

Brandling

Redworm

Snail

Shrimp

Nymph

Lobworm

Caddis grub

Caddis Larvae

■ Caddis grubs are present in many waters in the British Isles, both still and moving. They carry their own home with them in the form of a tube attached to the body, formed out of local materials which not only give protection, but act as camouflage. They attach themselves to water weed and this is one way of catching them – pulling or raking the weed out and then searching for the grubs. (64)

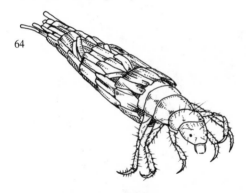

64

■ Another way to obtain grubs is by sinking weighted bunches of twigs into the water, or by suspending cabbage or brussels stumps overnight, collecting them the next day when the caddis larvae will have taken up residence. Never attempt to carry the grubs in water – lack of oxygen will quickly kill them. Instead, choose a large airtight plastic box and line the inside of this with wet weed before turning the grubs into it. Transported this way, they will keep for 12 hours or so.

■ When placing the grubs onto the hook remove the protective casing first, then lightly nick the point through the last segment of the body, leaving the head free. (65, 66)

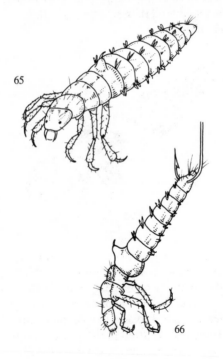

65

66

Caterpillars

■ A natural bait where bushes and trees
overhang the water, caterpillars can easily
be collected from the vegetable garden
during the early summer months and kept
in an aquarium with a supply of food until
required. Lightly hooked through the skin
and then dapped (fished in a breeze with an
unweighted line) at a rod's length from the
bank onto the surface of the water, they are
irresistible to chub and rudd. (67)

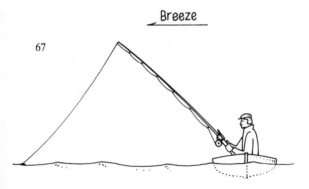

Crayfish

■ This crustacean is found in clear, pure,
running water throughout most of the
British Isles. The freshwater crayfish looks

and behaves exactly like its saltwater relative. (68)

68

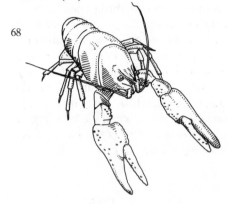

■ Trap crayfish with a drop net which has been baited with a piece of kipper or other fresh and tasty flesh. (69)

69

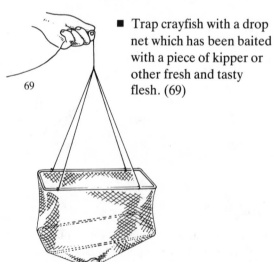

- Evening and early night is the best time for action. Drop the net and leave for several minutes, then raise steadily.

- Don't attempt to carry crayfish in water – instead use the wet weed method, as for caddis larvae.

- Tiny baits are best, mounted whole on a single hook. (70)

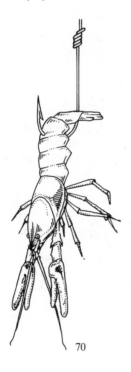

70

- The tail section, broken from a freshly killed crayfish, is another killing hookbait. But this method demands a large hook. (71)

71

Grasshoppers

- Easily gathered, grasshoppers should be kept in a small plastic bottle with air holes bored in its lid. From this they can be released one at a time. (72)

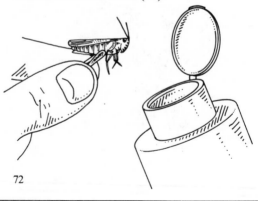

72

■ Mounted on a single hook
  they can be freelined and
  fished on the surface
  or allowed to swim
  in the stream.
  (73)

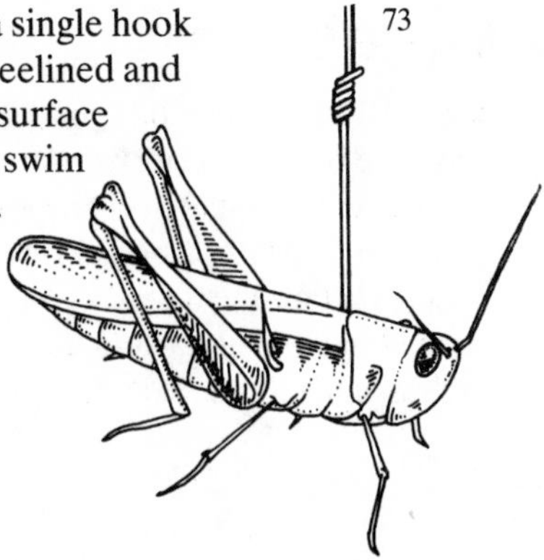

73

Leeches

■ Horse leeches are an excellent
  bait for bottom feeding fish –
  especially tench and carp.
  They can be sifted from
  mud on the bottom of
  the water and kept in an
  aquarium until required.
  Mount two or more at a
  time on a thin wire hook. (74)

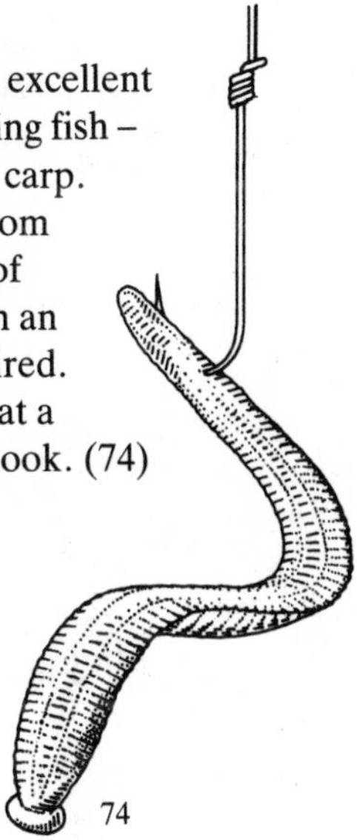

74

Mussels

■ Swan mussels can be found in shallow water beside the banks of rivers and enclosed waters. They stand on one end in the mud the other protruding out into the water. It takes little time to gather them. They can be kept in an aquarium until required. Transport them in damp moss. (75)

75

■ Use a strong knife slid into the hinged back of the shell to open the mussel. (76)

76

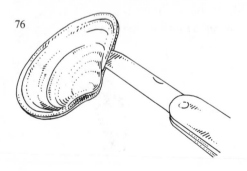

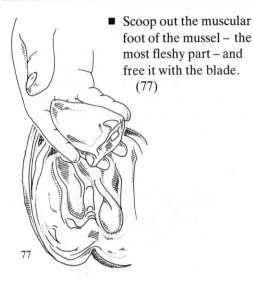

- Scoop out the muscular foot of the mussel – the most fleshy part – and free it with the blade. (77)

77

- Mount the bait onto a large hook, using the shells ground up and added to groundbait as an additional attractor. (78)

78

Shrimps

■ These small freshwater hoppers can be
  collected out of the thick blanket weed that
  proliferates in many waters. Larger shrimps
  can be mounted onto a small, fine wire hook
  and are especially killing when allowed to
  swim the stream. (79)

79

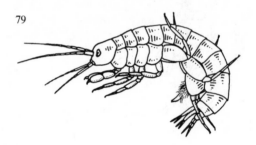

Silkweed

■ A traditional weir bait, where the fine green
  strands grow in flowing water on any of the
  fixtures and fittings just below the water
  level. Rub the weed free with a knife or the
  rim of a landing net and don't attempt to
  pull it away. Crushing will spoil its
  attractiveness and kill the small natural

insects in the weed that fish are looking for. (80)

80

- Keep the weed in water, in a plastic box. Bait the hook by drawing it through the weed and allowing it to catch to the shank of the hook. Don't squeeze or twist it on. Some anglers use a tiny triangle which baits more easily. (81)

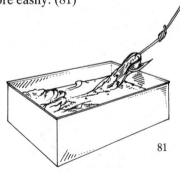

81

- Swim the stream using a big float that can
  be seen. Keep a tight line which will allow
  you to feel, as well as see a take. (82)

82

Slugs

- Once a supply of slugs have been gathered
  from the garden they can be kept in a moist
  aquarium, fed, and allowed to breed. This
  will give a supply of baits for a large part of
  the year. All colours of slug, red, black, and
  grey, are acceptable to fish, especially chub.
  (83)

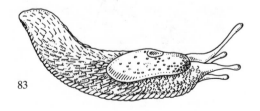

83

■ Take a supply to the waterside with a few lettuce leaves, contained in a plastic drum with a handle that can be attached to your belt. Also carry a large, old towel with which to clean your hands – slugs are sticky and slimy. Use a large (size 4) hook and impale the slug through the body. (84)

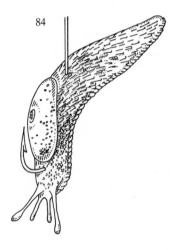

84

■ Freeline slugs, casting well upstream into weed and allowing the bait to work back on the stream, keeping a tight line. Chub especially will take this bait with considerable force.

Snails

- Ram's horn, pond and river snails are the bigger species that can be found feeding in weed clumps, and which make an excellent bait. Keep in an aquarium and carry in wet weed. (85)

85

- The hard shell is best crushed before mounted onto a hook. This will allow easy mounting.

Worms

- Everyone's idea of a fishing bait, whether an angler or not. Worms account for more fish during a year than any other bait – and will catch every species of fish. But catching and keeping worms is as important as fishing with them, especially if the angler wants the

worms to be available during summer when
drought drives them deep underground or
winter's cold keeps them from view.

■ There are three main species of worm that
are useful to the angler, they are the
lobworm, redworm and brandling.
Lobworms are by far the biggest in size and
can be identified by the large thick circle
that runs around the body. Redworms are
smaller, up to 4 in long, while brandlings,
similar in size to the redworm, can be
identified by a series of yellow rings that
encircle the red body. (86)

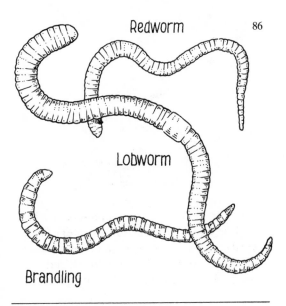

Redworm   86

Lobworm

Brandling

- Lobworms can be gathered from a lawn
  after dark, when they come to the surface.
  In dry weather a good watering helps to
  bring them up. The other two worm species
  are usually found in manure heaps or under
  stones and rotted branches on the ground.
  Once gathered, keep the worms in
  sphagnum moss (you can buy it at a florist)
  which is dampened down. Examine the
  worms each day and remove the dead ones,
  their presence quickly kills all the others.
  (87)

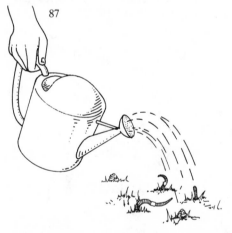

87

- It is easy to make a wormery of your own.
  Sink a large wooden box in a corner of the
  garden, make a few holes in the bottom for
  drainage and then fill this with soil and, if
  available, dead leaves and a little garden

refuse. Water it, place your worms on the soil and then cover completely with old, wet newspapers or a large plastic bag. Even in a heavy frost the worms will be ready to dig up.

■ Take care when you impale your worm on the hook. They are quickly stripped during a long cast – especially if a large worm has been put onto a small hook. Don't forget that it is possible to use two hooks, mounted one above the other or even a three-hook rig on which the worms can be fastened, showing them under the water in their full length, not just a jumbled and uninteresting ball. (88)

88

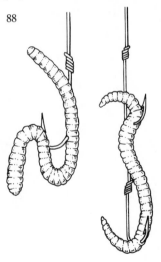

Bloodworms

- This tiny bait is not a worm at all but the
  larva of a gnat or midge. It is also known as
  tubifex and as such is obtained by aquarists
  as food for their pet fish. Due to the
  problems of collecting it, the bloodworm is
  not often on sale as an anglers' bait. The
  dedicated bloodworm angler will wade in
  thick mud to scrape the tiny larvae from its
  surface. (89)

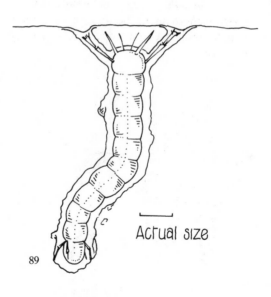

Actual size

89

- Due to their size, hooking bloodworms is not easy, the traditional method being to lay the thin, tiny larva on the ball of the thumb and impale it on a very fine, sharp hook. (90)

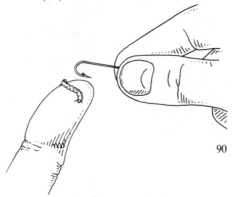

90

Maggots

- Probably the most popular bait used in coarse angling, maggots are best purchased from the tackle shop. It is possible to breed them, but it takes considerable skill and time to produce a really acceptable bait. Maggots for the hook are the larvae of the bluebottles and the largest in size. The greenbottle gives a maggot known as a pinkie, inferior to that of the bluebottle, while the common or garden housefly gives a small maggot known as a squatt, so

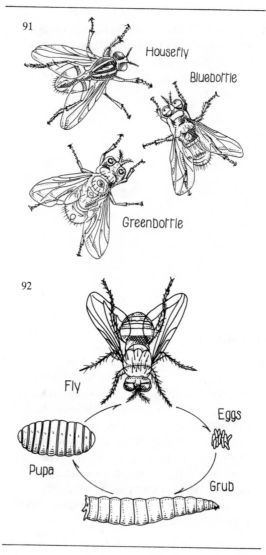

91 Housefly Bluebottle Greenbottle

92 Fly Eggs Grub Pupa

insignificant that it generally finishes up with the pinkie being used as groundbait. (91, 92)

- Maggots that are not kept properly will soon pupate and turn into casters, which are a bait in their own right. Collect maggots from the shop in a ventilated box and immediately store them in the fridge until they are required. Kept like this they will remain motionless and last for several days. Two days before use, sieve them to remove all sawdust and unwanted material in which they may have been packed. There is an excellent purpose-built sieve on the market that will do this. Once separated, turn the maggots out on to fine sand and leave them to work through this for 24 hours while they further cleanse themselves. (93)

93

- Then sieve the maggots once more, freeing them of sand. Turn them into bran or oatmeal which will polish them and help free them of grease – which causes them to float – and keep them in this until they are used.

- Hook the maggot through the blunt end, where the two black spots are, and not the sharp end. This will allow it to wriggle attractively in the water. (94)

94

Casters

- The dark-coloured caster, which is the chrysalid of the maggot, is a seductive bait that can be bred or purchased from the tackle shop.

- It takes six days for a maggot to turn into a caster. Maggots that are separated and turned out into clean material should be tipped into a tin or box so that they cover the bottom to a depth of an inch or so. Keep them in a cool place and watch them daily. When the first caster appears, turn the maggots into a sieve and allow them to work through and back into their original box. Casters only will be left in the sieve. Repeat this process as often as necessary.

■ When sufficient quantities have been separated and collected, drop them into a bowl of water. Those that float have no great use and should be discarded and flushed away. Those remaining should be packed into a plastic bag and stored again in the fridge, ready for use.

■ Hook the caster through the end, turning the point and bend so that it lodges in the body of the chrysalid itself. Use a fine-wire hook. (95)

95

Wasp and Docken Grubs

- The wasp grub is another maggot, of a sort, but a much larger and sweeter grub. It is a traditional countryman's bait that has accounted for many specimen-sized fish. But collecting this grub is a hazardous business and should not be attempted by poking about in a wasp nest! There are chemical methods, but these must only be used after expert advice and then under supervision. As its name implies, the docken grub is found in the roots of that plant. It is a very soft, segmented bait and it is difficult to avoid spoiling it when hooking. Very fine wire hooks are needed, the sharp barb being inserted just nicked into the skin. (96)

96

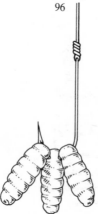

BAIT ADDITIVES

There are a large number of additives that may be mixed with practically any hookbait. We have already discussed the use of blancmange powder, sugar, and soda when we prepared some of the baits described above. There are many more, some good, some indifferent. Many anglers believe that there must be one super-secret additive that will bring every species of fish on to immediate and savage feed. There is no such miracle substance! But there are many additives that bring success when used sensibly and with consideration of the time of year, water and bait. The subject attained a kind of cult image a few years ago, with closely guarded 'secret' formulae being devised.

Various essences used in cooking such as vanilla, almond and so on, are some, aniseed is another, that were thought at one time to be deadly. Bovril, Oxo, Marmite all help, especially with meat-type baits. Honey is yet another tried additive together with treacle. They can bring success to fish with a 'sweet tooth', such as carp. Pilchard oil, oil of geranium, blood from the abattoir – all have their day. It is up to the angler to experiment and blend to get the most from what is available. (97)

97

COCKTAIL BAITS

Cocktail baits are two or more items gathered on the same hook – virtually a sandwich – which can improve a single attractiveness. There are endless permutations, but a few examples could be a maggot added behind a piece of crust, imparting movement to it as it swims the stream; cheese mounted behind meat – the lightness of the cheese constrasting with the dark of the meat; maggot and caster, again light and dark. When making a cocktail bait aim always to improve the single bait you are using.

GROUNDBAITS

A general rule of thumb for groundbaits is to remember that light, powder-type groundbaits are used for stillwaters and those that are slow flowing. Heavy groundbaits are used in fast flowing waters or those where it is necessary to cast or throw the bait over a distance from the bankside.

- Traditionally, light groundbaits are made from dried bread, ground either in a mincer or pounded into crumbs. Alternatives are biscuits, crumbed down, or some of the commercial products such as sausage rusk, bran, crushed oats. (98)

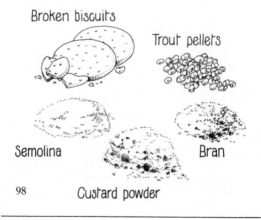

Broken biscuits

Trout pellets

Semolina

Bran

98   Custard powder

■ Heavy groundbaits have bread as a base, soaked and then stiffened with the addition of bran, brewers' grains, cattle feed – any bulk substance that will help the bread to be moulded into heavy balls that can be thrown over a distance and which will sink rapidly.

■ Groundbaits are best mixed at the waterside and a canvas bucket is ideal for both carrying and mixing in. (99)

99   Maggots

Flour   Sweetcorn

■ Many additives can be used to improve the basic groundbait. Examples are legion. The water in which hempseed has been boiled helps to add attraction, as does the seed itself when it has been dried, crushed and mixed into the groundbait base. Potatoes boiled and mashed, then added to a heavy groundbait give an exceptional mix useful for floodwaters and the angler who wishes to use par-boiled potato as bait. Cheese ground with a hand grater and added to the mix, sausage meat, blood, all help to give attraction and to tempt fish close to whatever hookbait the angler may be using.

- Finally there are loose groundbaits, basically offerings of the hookbait thrown into the swim or broadcast around it. Small pellets of paste, loose hemp grains, a few cubes of luncheon meat – all advertise the presence of food. But groundbait should never be offered in such quantities that the fish feed on it while the angler's baited hook is overlooked as it lies on the bottom. (100)

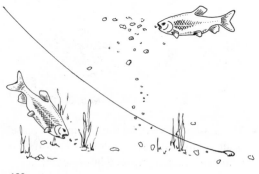

100

PART IV
FLOAT AND LEGER RIGS

It is safe to say that every coarse angler starts his career by fishing with a float and it is only some time later that there comes the understanding that there is another method called legering.

In this section the float in its various forms is discussed and the conditions under which each one is used. Water, weather and fish species all play their part in arriving at the most useful float for the session ahead.

The second part of this section deals with fishing without a float: legering. There are some water conditions where the use of a float is nigh impossible, or where the feeding habits of the fish species sought necessitate the bait being on the bottom.

7 FLOATS, WEIGHTS AND RIGS

INTRODUCTION

That most anglers use a float when they fish is not surprising: the float is a focal point where action might occur, the means of knowing when a fish is interested in the bait and – even more important – a final indication that the bait has been taken into the fish's mouth, the moment to strike. Most anglers use a float because of the ease with which it records the bite. The float leger, the pure leger and even free-lining are equally efficient styles in catching fish, but their use demands more skill from the angler in recognising a bite, then assessing what the fish is doing with the bait.

Some anglers go through their fishing lives using only two or three types of float to cover every need, regardless of the water being fished, the species sought or the season and it is a recipe for disaster. The float to be used must be decided on after a number of facts have been examined and considered. On the other hand there is no need for the vast array of floats one sees in the tackle shops or occasionally beside the angler at the waterside.

Is the float really necessary? Some of the reasons have been given above, the most important being that the float records a bite from a fish. But that is not all. For instance, it is often possible to identify the fish that is interested in the bait. The dashing, grabbing bite of a perch is one example: the sudden lift, then collapse of the float horizontally on the surface, followed by a lift and slow drag under is the unmistakable hallmark of a bream bite. Lightning stabs at the float usually indicate a dace, while there is no mistaking the sucking, delicate bite from a tench, making the float slowly wobble and gyrate. With this knowledge the angler soon knows that it is not necessary to strike immediately at the first twitch of the float, sometimes it is prudent to wait on the alert for the fish to swim away with the bait.

So, by studying float movements a picture can be built up of what is happening under the surface. In simple terms, the float records attention. This attention is sometimes unwelcome, as when a small nuisance perch pulls at the bait, the hook or line becomes caught on the bottom, or on an underwater snag, but again the angler soon recognises this as something separate from a bite and reacts accordingly.

Just as important as indicating attention is the ability of the float to carry and direct a bait. There are several ways in which this can be done and the angler must take full advantage of them. For instance, the float can hold a bait clear of the bottom, which will prevent snagging, perhaps tangling in weed; more usually the float holds the bait so that it can be recognised as edible and taken by a fish.

A float can use the current to carry the bait to where the angler considers a fish to be lying. Swimming the stream, where the float (with the baited hook) is carried along with the current, is an example. By holding the line back, or by moving the rod tip, the angler can manoeuvre the float – and with it the bait – to reach specific areas, such as underwater roots close to the bank where a fish may be lying.

Finally, the wind can be used to move the float and carry a bait. This is particularly useful in stillwaters where even a small float, together with the line, will sweep a bait into a place inaccessible to the angler by normal casting. Recently, pike anglers have been taking advantage of the wind and special floats with adjustable and interchangeable sails have been produced that will drift a balanced bait across large distances.

Recording a bite is not the only piece of underwater information that the float gives. It also informs the angler of the exact location of the bait – and that information can be invaluable. Perhaps an underwater hot-spot has been found, say a ridge or hole where fish are lying and where they are interested in feeding. It is the float and its position which tells the angler whether the cast has been successful or not.

In a similar way the float provides information about a hooked fish while it is being played, especially when fishing in deep water. With the float above the surface the direction it takes can show where a fish is heading and approximately how far it is below the surface.

On arrival at the bank and intending to use a float, the angler should stop and think, not reach blindly for that old favourite, or one regarded as a lucky charm.

The Water

Whether the water has movement or not will influence the type of float to be selected. If the water is still, the first consideration must be a small float that will land quietly on the water and present little or no resistance to a taking fish. If the water is moving, strength of current will dictate the size of float to be used.

If the intention is to lay-on, or hold a float still in the current a slim float must be selected. For trotting, allowing the float to ride along with the current, a float substantial in length and circumference will be needed to pull line from the reel.

With depth, movement must be also be considered. Using a large float in shallow water is counter-productive. Colour of the water is also a consideration: in gin-clear streams the float above the bait can be seen. (1)

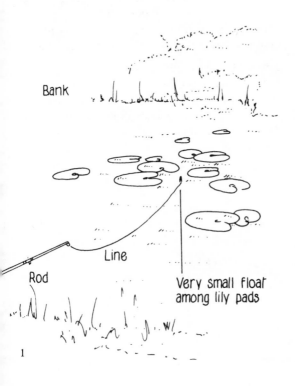

Bank

Line

Rod

Very small float among lily pads

1

The Weather

Wind and rain are the float fisherman's two main enemies, both making casting difficult and, by disturbing the surface of the water, creating problems with visibility and drag. Again, the angler must select the float to suit the occasion. A heavy float and the weight necessary to cock it will prevent line cling (nylon sticking to the surface of the rod) and help to achieve distance when the cast is made.

The angler's visibility can be assisted in difficult conditions by the use of windbeaters, floats with a small round knob or beacon on their tips which stand high above the surface of the water and can be seen for a considerable distance.

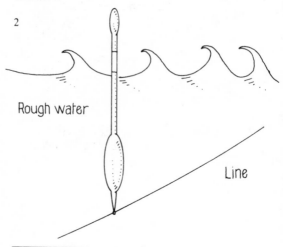

2

Rough water

Line

To some extent, drag can be controlled, but not entirely beaten, by various float attachments. Generally, by using a suitable float, the line can be fastened to it below the surface, which helps to keep the float (and bait) in one position. (2)

The Fish

Size, feeding habits and habitat will govern float selection. This is common-sense although there are anglers who try to compromise with a float entirely unsuited to the species that the angler will *not* be catching!

Under normal circumstances, roach, rudd and dace need a delicate float. Pike require a large, streamlined float that will move away with a fish without it feeling resistance. For grayling, tradition requires a small ducker-type of float designed to cope with the shallow and moving waters these fish inhabit. All these requirements, of course, can be over-ridden by weather conditions and casting distance. (3)

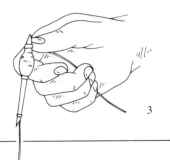

3

Casting

With floats, size, diameter, weight, shape, all
can influence the casting distance, or the way
that a cast must be made. But remember, when
the float is selected the angler must make sure
that the terminal tackle in general (i.e. line,
hook link) will be in balance with it. Heavy
shotting patterns needed to make bulky floats
work can cause havoc with fine nylon. (4)

The Light

Near-darkness of dawn and dusk, bright
sunlight, the haze of mists that cling to the
water – all these and more must be contended
with if the float-fisherman wants to see every
movement of the float. The shape of the float
often controls its visibility but usually the
colour of the tip is more likely to be seen. This

means changing to a different float, sometimes several times within a short space of time, but it must be done. Light colours against dark backgrounds, special paints, even floats with an illuminated tip, are found in the angler's tackle-box, and with commonsense can be used to good result. (5)

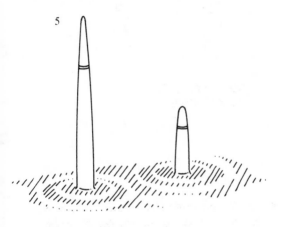

5

Adaptability

The trap of sticking to one float has been mentioned, and the need of the angler to be prepared to move from one type or colour to another quickly and easily. Some floats allow quick change, some do not. This, therefore, is the time to consider the various means of attaching floats to the line.

■ The traditional method of attaching float to
line is by means of an eye whipped on to the
float's tip. It is certain of doing so, but it
also means that shot and hook will have to
be removed if a change is to be made,
something difficult in poor light conditions.
(6)

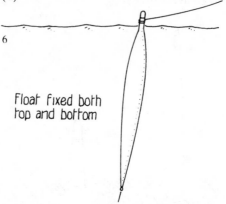

6

Float fixed both
top and bottom

■ But the eye end can be used to fasten the
line to the float so that the depth can be
altered easily – simply by taking two turns
around the wire, without securing line to
the top end. (7)

Line looped

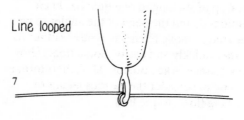

7

- Another possibility with the plain loop is to secure it with two small shot, one either side. Again, this leaves the tip free. (8)

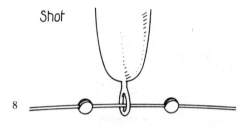

- A commercial quick-release attachment fastens by means of a sliding sleeve to the eye end. Expensive but reliable. (9)

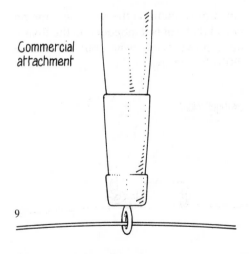

■ For the d-i-y angler there is the thin wire held by two pieces of insulating flex. Simple, cheap, but not foolproof. (10)

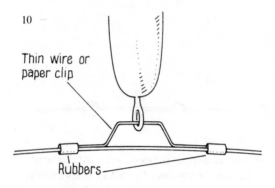

10

Thin wire or paper clip

Rubbers

■ An improvement on the wire eye is the tiny swivel that can be embedded in the float's tip. It prevents line twist – but still remains difficult to change. (11)

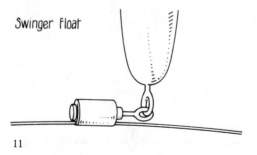

Swinger float

11

■ Float-rubbers are the traditional method of attachment, but they can perish, stretch and slip from the body of the float, thus loosening it. However, many anglers swear by *and at* them. (12)

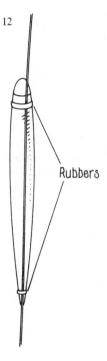

12

Rubbers

■ Moulded sleeves fit over the end of the float stem and provide a quick and easy means of change-over – providing there is room between the body of the float and the end of the stem itself. Where quick changes have to be made it is better than the plain wire ring. (13)

Moulded rubber sleeve

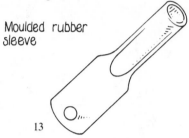

13

■ The fastest method of float-changing is by using a spring-clip attachment. This small wire spring has a loop at one end for the line. The larger bend at its other end fits through the ring in the float and the tiny plastic sleeve then slides down to grip the spring tight shut. Changes can be made in seconds. (14)

Spring clip float attachment

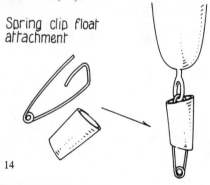

14

Storing Floats

Many of today's floats are fragile and need
protection while they are being carried in the
tackle bag — not just from breakage, but from
being chipped and cracked. Many anglers use
cigar-boxes or something similar, but the best
containers are proper padded and sectioned
wooden boxes obtainable from tackle shops:
each float is kept separate from the others and
can be selected quickly. (15)

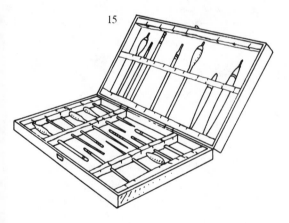

15

Making Floats

Anglers can easily make their own floats. The
tools needed are few, a sharp knife, files, glass-
paper, glue, varnish and paint. Materials are
easily obtainable and inexpensive: balsa wood

and fine dowelling from crafts shop, straws,
stiff bristles, tooth-picks, bottle corks — many
items are free and plentiful. Feathers can be
obtained from farmyards, game dealers, and
of course from country walks. There is a range
of good float kits on the market supplying
ready shaped materials that just need
assembling. (16)

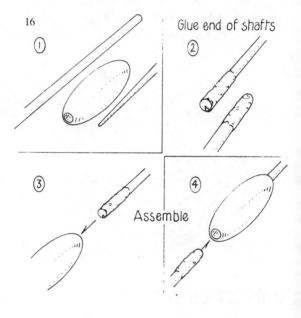

16

① ② Glue end of shafts

③ Assemble ④

FLOAT PATTERNS

The many shapes and sizes of floats are designed for certain jobs. The principal patterns are listed here with a brief description of the type of fishing they cover.

Quills

- Once the only type of float, quills are the simplest of all and still are among the cheapest and best. They include quills from the swan, goose, duck, crow, pheasant, peacock and porcupine, some you can no longer buy. Those most in use today include the porcupine and the peacock, the latter a favourite because it can be cut into lengths to suit the water. Cork bodies can be added to the quills, making floats capable of carrying a lot of weight. But the value of the simple quill lies in its delicacy, typified by the small crow-quill that can be fixed to the line by either end, and is sensitive enough to record the faint bites from a tench. At the other extreme is the goose quill, often used to make sliding floats for fishing deep water. (17)

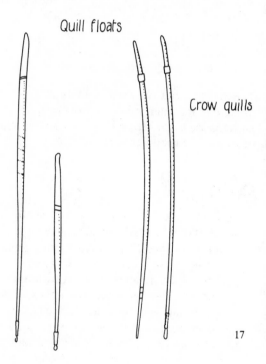

Quill floats

Crow quills

17

Avon Floats

- Excellent floats for long trotting, in other words allowing the bait to run downstream while pulling line from the reel, with the angler firmly in control and ready to strike.

It takes its name from the River Avon,
where the fast flow requires a big, but
delicate float. But the Avon float is equally
useful on the Thames and Severn. High on
the long stem, the balsa body is the secret of
this float's success, the weights required to
cock it keeping the float well down onto the
water. This enables the angler to 'hold back'
on the line, keeping the bait in front of the
float, not trailing behind, from where it is
nearly impossible to register a bite. Even
though the float may be lying nearly flat on
the surface of the water, the small but
sensitive tip above the body will always
register the slightest attention. (18)

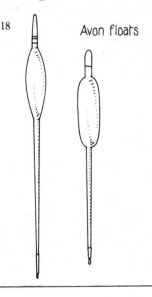

18   Avon floats

Balsa Floats

■ These are designed for really tough
conditions, rivers that are in flood, or where
the deep, boiling water of a swim would
play havoc with smaller and more sensitive
floats. But the balsa is not insensitive. The
secret of sensitivity in any float lies with the
size and thickness of that part which
protrudes from the surface of the water.
And if you look at the balsa family, the tip
is small and thin making the slightest touch
evident. Nor does size present problems
when casting, the streamlined body cutting
the air with the minimum of drag. It is
possible to cast long distances and still see
this all-wood float. Smaller models are very
successful in turbulent, shallow water such
as parts of weirpools — remaining in view
where thinner floats would be sucked under.
(19)

Stick Floats

■ Designed for running water where there is
an even flow, the swim not more than 6 ft
deep, stick floats do not work efficiently on
waters that are still, slow or very fast. They
will cope well with an upstream wind, but
fail badly if the wind turns downstream or
ruffles the surface of the swim, conditions

that drive the float (and the bait) too fast through the swim. Construction includes a balsa body mounted on a thin dowel or cane stem. The stick float is designed so that the tip only shows, the float riding vertically through the swim, when bites are recorded by complete disappearance. (20)

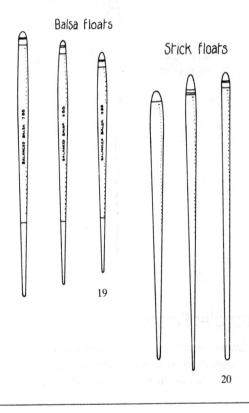

Balsa floats

Stick floats

19

20

- One variation of the stick float uses a wire instead of wood. The wire keeps the float riding easily and in a vertical position, the thin stem keeping water resistance to a minimum and allowing the float to run smoothly through the swim. (21)

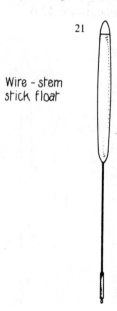

21

Wire - stem
stick float

Waggler Floats

- Universal floats, at home on most waters, wagglers are fastened to the line by one end only. They come in all shapes and sizes, the bigger and thicker models being designed to carry more weight. Most wagglers are constructed from peacock-quill stems, bodies being added from cork, balsa, and polystyrene. They are quick and easy to make and provide a good selection for the tackle box. In its plain form the waggler is secured to the line with a shot either side of the end eye, the line being sunk below the surface. (22)

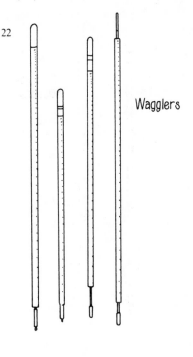

22

Wagglers

- Variations on the wagglers embody a fat body mounted onto the last third of the stem, which helps to steady it without preventing a delicate bite from being registered. A further advantage of this construction is that is slows the float through the water, keeping the bait moving at a taking speed. (23)

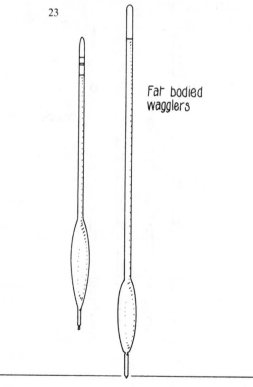

23

Fat bodied wagglers

■ Very large wagglers with enlarged bulbs at their end, sometimes over 12 in long, would need a mountain of shot to make them work. For this reason they are weighted with pieces of brass mounted into the body and glued into position. Weight on the line is kept to a minimum, further weight being used with advantage to make extra-long casts. (24)

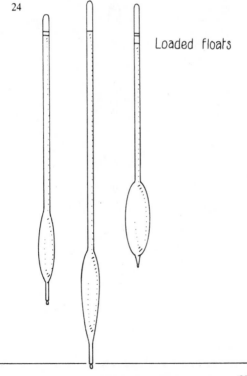

24

Loaded floats

■ Windbeaters are another branch of the
waggler family used when high winds drive
the waves roaring down the water. Standing
well above the surface, the beacon on the
tip remains relatively steady and helps the
angler to assess a bite. The thin stem slices
through the water making the float very
delicate despite being 10 in or more long.
(25)

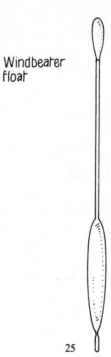

Windbeater
float

25

Slider Floats

- For use in deep waters, these floats, as the name suggests, slide down the line until a predetermined place is reached where a stop knot has been set, preventing further sinking of the bait and cocking the float. Many anglers use an ordinary float, setting the stop knot so that it will be held at the end ring, and attaching the float to the line by that loop only. But this method is not as successful as the float properly constructed to slide. Remember that the slider can present a bait both on and off the bottom. (26)

26

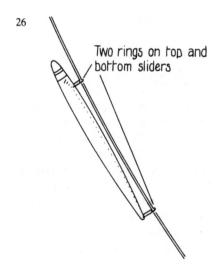

Two rings on top and bottom sliders

- The sliding float is only successful when the correct stop knot has been used. This diagram shows how it should be tied. (27)

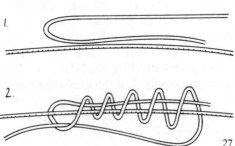

Antennae Floats

- These are great floats for general fishing where there is movement on the water. The thin stick that cuts the surface is unmoved as waves pass over it but because of the balance of the body, the float — and the bait — remains still and not bobbing up and down. It is from this float, one of angling's golden oldies, that the waggler developed. Unlike the waggler, attached at the bottom end only, this float is fastened at top and bottom. (28)

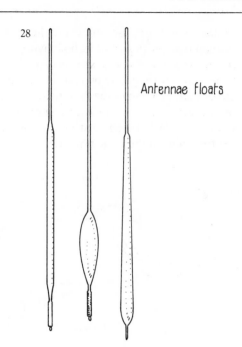

28

Antennae floats

Bubble Floats

- These are transparent, plastic bubbles that have a small hole sealed with a plug in the side allowing them to be filled with water, making weight for casting. Originally designed for use when fly fishing, the bubble float lay on the surface and acted as a controller for the fly which could be manoeuvred into positions not normally reached. In coarse fishing it is used in very shallow water, or positions where the normal float, with part of its body lying under the surface, would arouse suspicion. Line passes through the two eyed loops at either end, and allows the float to be pushed up and down in the same way as a normal float. Useful where long distance is needed, yet freelining at the same time. (29)

29   Bubble floats

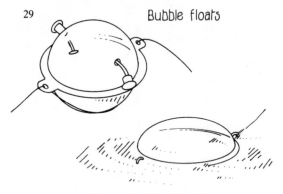

Streamlined bubble float

Pole Floats

■ Designed for use with ultra fine lines and hooks, pole floats are strong weapons in the match-angler's armoury. Adopted from the Continent, pole floats feature a strong and rather outsized body which gives stability for casting and, sunk below the surface, hold the bait steady. Their needle-fine stems can just be seen as a tiny whisker protruding through the surface, presenting no resistance to a taking fish and recording the most delicate of bites. (30)

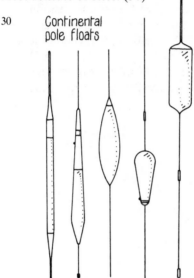

30   Continental pole floats

■ Because pole floats are so delicate, anglers make them up at home and transport them on plastic winders ready for mounting or changing as required. (31)

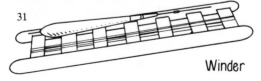

31

Winder

Night Lights

■ There have been various attempts at
producing a float that can be seen during
night fishing. But the best is probably the
Betanyte, which houses a tiny tritium-
powered light tip that lasts for years, and
glows with a strong light no matter how
dark the night might be. There are similar
models on the market, all on the same
principle. Float fishing during darkness is

32

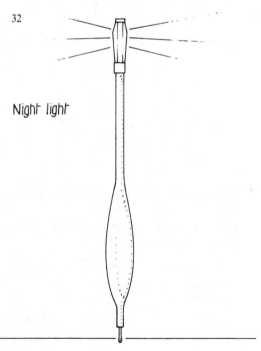

Night light

not easy, the float can often be taken away by a slowly moving fish without the angler being aware of it. This float is at its best when seen against a contrasting background when movement can be seen. (32)

Bungs

- Originally the leading float for pike anglers, the bung has now been eclipsed by modern, streamlined models that do not present its resistance to a taking fish. The *Fishing Gazette* model led the field for years and is still available. (33)

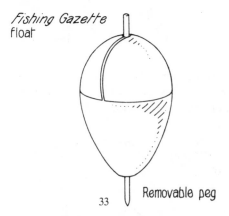

Fishing Gazette float

Removable peg

33

- Modern pike floats are mostly sliders called 'cigars' for obvious reasons, the line being led through the centre of the float's body and stopped by a stop knot. The type of water and the size of the bait govern the size of the float. (34)

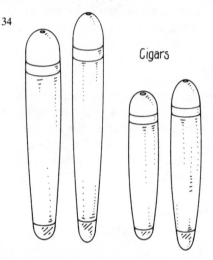

34

Cigars

■ Some pike men believe that the use of a tiny pilot float gives less resistance to a taking fish and these are popular. (35)

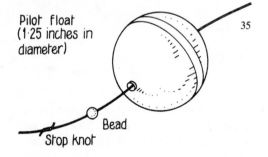

Pilot float
(1·25 inches in
diameter)

35

Bead

Stop knot

WEIGHTS FOR FLOAT FISHING

Weight is necessary when float fishing to make it stand up and show above the surface, and to help in making a cast. The amount needed depends on the type of water to be fished, the float that has been selected and the style of fishing decided upon. Until recently the line was weighted by lead shot, but legislation now prevents its use because of allegations that it poisons bird life. Under the Control of Pollution (Anglers' Lead Weights) Regulations 1986 the importation and sale of lead weights below 1oz was prohibited, and the angler's traditional split-shot usage was no more. There are now a number of substitutes on the market with the mass and appearance of the traditional lead shot and where the terms 'split shot', 'shot' or 'lead(s)' are used these refer to lead substitutes and not traditional lead shot.

- ■ Shot for weighting the line is split, allowing it to be cramped together. Softness is essential or it will damage the line as it is squeezed. Examine and select the best of

the artificial lead substitutes that are
available in the tackle shop. (36)

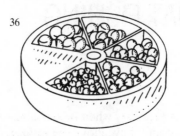

36

■ Shot is sized, the numbers used to describe
the size running in descending order. The
same method of shot description is used by
those who shoot, so some of their
terminology has crept into angling. Biggest
is swan-shot, followed by AAA, BB, No. 4,
6, 8 and so on. Size 10 is probably the
smallest, but there are some smaller still —
usually used in pole fishing. (37)

Split shot (actual size)

	Number per ounce		
SSG ⬭ 15	170 ◔ 4		
AAA ◔ 35	220 ◔ 5		
BB ◔ 70	270 ◔ 6		
1 ◔ 100	340 ◔ 7		
3 ◔ 140	450 ◔ 8		

37

■ Most modern floats have the weight needed
  to cock them marked along the body,
  otherwise trial and error have to find the
  shot required to make the float work. (38)

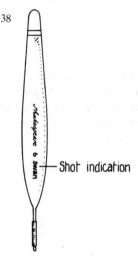

Shot indication

Weighting Patterns

■ Attaching shot on to the line in any order or
  position is bad fishing and will not make the
  float work properly. There is no guarantee
  that the bait will be where it should be, and
  it could even restrict the distance of the
  cast. Patterns, the placing of shot, are
  important and the principal ones are
  introduced in the next chapter, with an
  explanation of the various fishing styles.

FLOAT-FISHING STYLES

The float can be used in stillwater or in the flow of the current and the styles described here are those well-proven traditional methods found to be suitable for the varying conditions the angler finds.

39

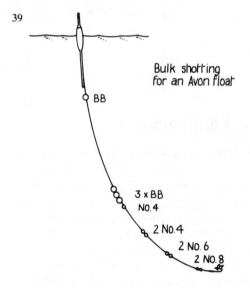

Bulk shotting
for an Avon float

BB

3 x BB
NO. 4

2 NO. 4

2 NO. 6

2 NO. 8

Trotting

■ A general term that describes a bait carried along with the current. Another description is swimming the stream. The bait must precede the float or a bite will not register. The shotting pattern for use with the Avon float is shown. (39)

■ A trotting pattern for water with a slower flow is shown, using a stick float. (40)

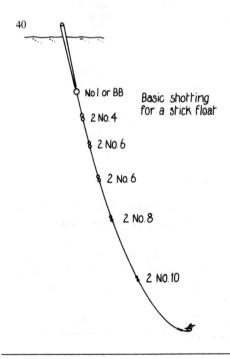

40

No I or BB

Basic shotting for a stick float

2 No. 4

2 No. 6

2 No. 6

2 No. 8

2 No. 10

- Where the water moves quickly but strong
  wind is creating a fast drag across the
  surface, use this pattern with a large
  waggler. (41)

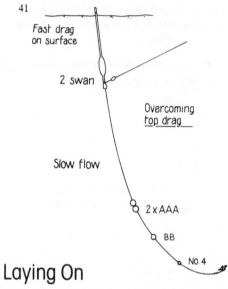

41

Fast drag
on surface

2 swan

Overcoming
top drag

Slow flow

2 x AAA

BB

No. 4

Laying On

- In this style, the bait is allowed to lay on the
  bottom and is kept there with a small weight
  while the float lies at an angle, ready to
  record the smallest bite, the line between it
  and the bottom shot tight. Almost any float
  can be used for this rig which is usually
  practised in stationary or slow-moving
  water. Here the rig shows a waggler,
  fastened at the bottom end only which

allows the line to be sunk below the surface,
an assistance in avoiding drag where there
is any wind. (42)

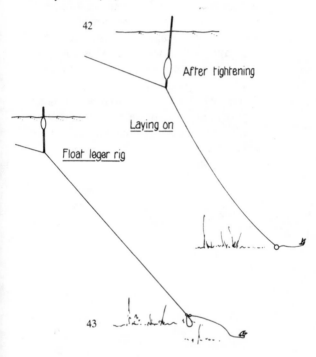

- Another method of laying on, float-
  legering, uses a leger weight instead of a
  small shot on the bottom. This rig allows
  long casting and is delicate and responsive
  to bites in spite of its rather clumsy
  appearance. (43)

289

Stret-Pegging

■ This is a style of laying on with the angler
using the current to work the bait round
from just in front, to a position against the
bank downstream of his swim. The rod must
constantly be held because bites are often
fast — sometimes with such force that fish
practically hook themselves. The ordinary
Avon rig is used but the float is adjusted so
that the length between it and the hook is
greater than the depth to be fished. This
keeps the bait scraping the river bed at all
times. (44)

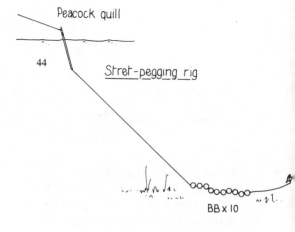

Peacock quill

44   Stret-pegging rig

BB x 10

Lift Method

- By attaching a float by the end only and keeping weight to a minimum a float will lift and lay it on its side when a fish takes the bait. It is done by having the largest shot just resting on the bottom and keeping a short link between it and the bait. An excellent stillwater rig. (45)

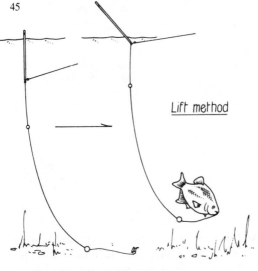

45

Lift method

When the bait is taken, the bottom weight is lifted and the float rises

Drop Method

- Allowing the bait to sink slowly in still
  waters is a certain way of catching roach,
  rudd and similar species. A tiny waggler
  cocked by the finest shot will allow that
  slow drop of the bait that fish cannot resist.
  (46)

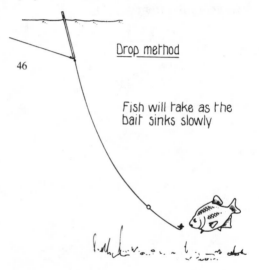

Drop method

Fish will take as the
bait sinks slowly

46

- Drop-fishing needs careful groundbaiting, a
  cloud groundbait gets the best results. Be
  careful not to make the cloud groundbait
  too much of a feed, thus spoiling the
  chances of the hookbait. Any kind of
  groundbait must attract — not feed the fish.
  (47)

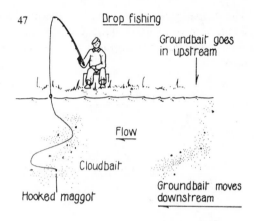

■ Try sinking the bait quickly after a period of drop fishing, because bigger fish may be below those that you are catching. This shotting pattern will get the bait down past smaller fish in double-quick time. (48)

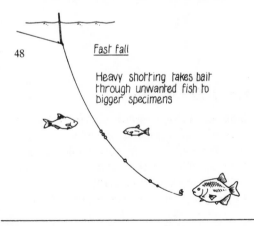

■ The drop method can be used in running
water with good effect. This slow-sinking
rig using an Avon float shows how to fish it.
(49)

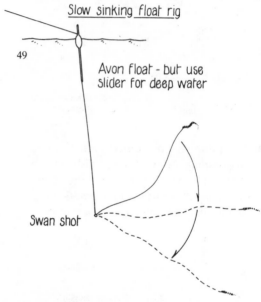

Slow sinking float rig

49

Avon float - but use
slider for deep water

Swan shot

Sink-and-Draw ·

■ Sink-and-draw is a method of attracting the
fish by moving the bait instead of waiting
for a fish to find it. Instead of a float, one
shot is pinched on to the line above the bait
with enough weight to enable a cast to be
made. The bait is allowed to sink and then

worked back to the angler in a series of
jerks. (50)

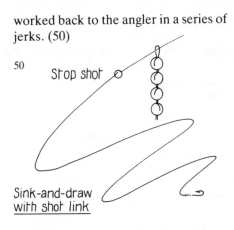

50

Stop shot

Sink-and-draw
with shot link

■ Another method of sink-and-draw is by the
use of a bubble float. This assists bite
detection through movement from the float.
But with the sink-and-draw style the best
bite detection is by feel. (51)

Sink-and-draw with bubble float

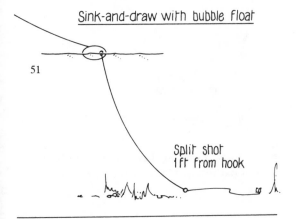

51

Split shot
1ft from hook

Sliding-Float Rigs

- Fishing the bait off the bottom demands the shot pattern to be well above the bait. This rig is using a waggler secured through the end ring only. (52)

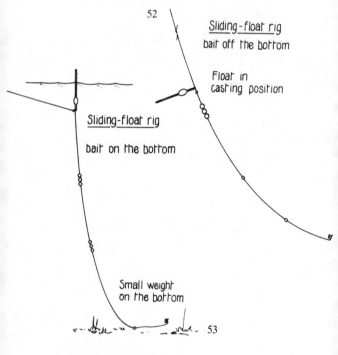

52

Sliding-float rig
bait off the bottom

Float in
casting position

Sliding-float rig

bait on the bottom

Small weight
on the bottom

53

- For fishing with the bait on the bottom, the shot pattern is split with one shot resting on the bed. (53)

Stick Floats

- Many anglers kill the sensitivity of this float by using too much weight. In shotting with the stick the secret is 'small and plenty', as this diagram of a representative stick-float rig shows. (54)

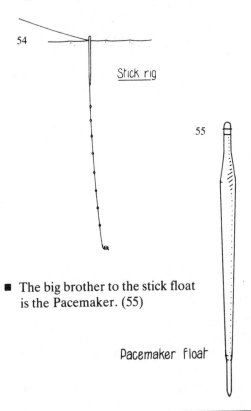

54

Stick rig

55

- The big brother to the stick float is the Pacemaker. (55)

Pacemaker float

■ A heavyweight for heavy water conditions, the shotting pattern for the Pacemaker takes time to put in place, but keeps the bait down. (56)

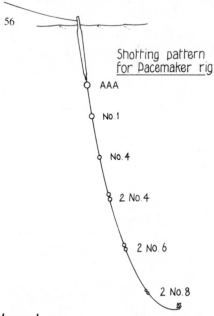

56

Shotting pattern for Pacemaker rig

AAA

No.1

No.4

2 No.4

2 No.6

2 No.8

Wagglers

■ Wagglers are secured by the ring end only. One possible method is by using a dust shot each side of the ring itself. But care must be taken or the float won't pull under on the bite. The incorrect way is shown here, with the shots close against the ring, preventing movement of the float to indicate a bite. (57)

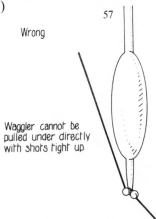

57

Wrong

Waggler cannot be pulled under directly with shots tight up

■ The correct way, leaving a gap between the shot and the float allows it to hang and dip when the bait is taken. (58)

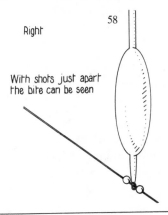

58

Right

With shots just apart the bite can be seen

■ This shot pattern allows a slow-sinking bait, often taken by fish as it falls. (59)

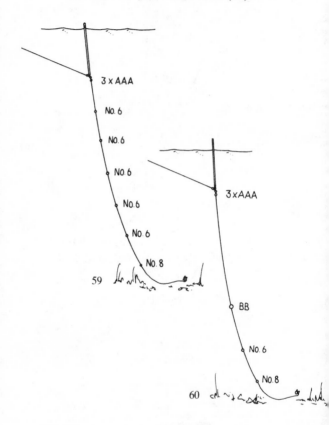

■ For a more rapid sinking of the bait use this pattern, concentrating weight at the bottom end. (60)

■ Buoyant baits, such as crust, will need even
more weight to keep them on the bottom.
This shotting pattern is ideal for the
purpose. (61)

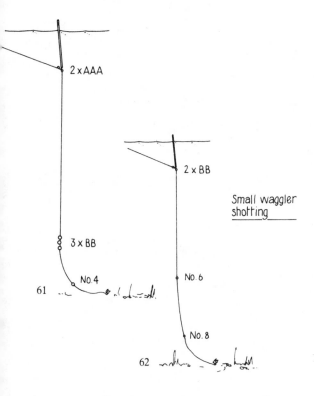

2 × AAA

2 × BB

Small waggler
shotting

3 × BB

No.4

61

No.6

No.8

62

■ For very confined waters that require small
floats this shotting pattern is recommended.
(62)

■ Occasionally it is necessary to slow a bait
down while swimming the stream. This
pattern trails the bait and holds back the
float. (63)

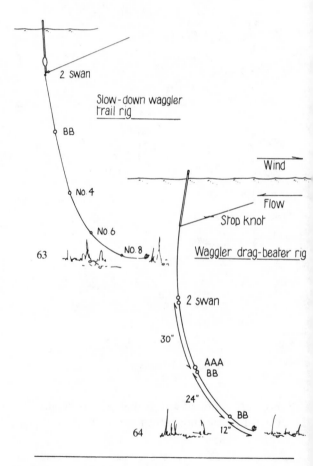

Slow-down waggler
trail rig

2 swan

BB

No. 4

No 6

63   No. 8

Wind

Flow

Stop knot

Waggler drag-beater rig

2 swan

30"

AAA
BB

24"

BB

64   12"

■ When the wind is against the current a drag is created which causes the float to ride around on the surface. Here is a pattern and style to combat those conditions. (64)

Float Paternoster

■ A deadly way of anchoring a bait in one position and keeping it off the bottom. It is usual^ly used with a small livebait for perch and fished roving-style, the angler moving along the bank casting into likely places. (65)

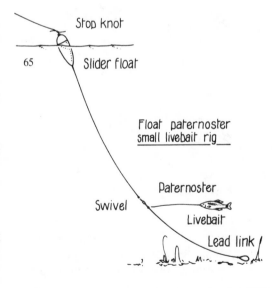

Stop knot

65 Slider float

Float paternoster
small livebait rig

Paternoster

Swivel Livebait

Lead link

Pole Float Rigs

■ Shotting these tiny floats is an art in itself.
The weights are minute and there is a
special cramp for fastening them to the line.
The larger sizes, called Olivetti leads, are
usually pear shaped and hollow so they can
be threaded down the line. Other small
leger weights are Styl leads and Mouse
Droppings (because of their unpleasant
resemblance in shape and size!). They are
less likely to tangle than strings of shot. (66)

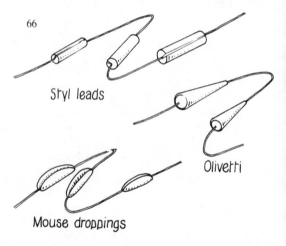

66

Styl leads

Olivetti

Mouse droppings

■ The pole float is shotted until the fine stem
just breaks the water. Two methods of
shotting are shown, one for a Teardrop

float, the other for what is known as a
Carrot. (67, 68)

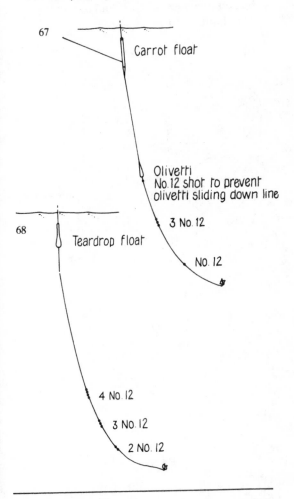

67

Carrot float

Olivetti
No. 12 shot to prevent
olivetti sliding down line

3 No. 12

No. 12

68

Teardrop float

4 No. 12

3 No. 12

2 No. 12

■ It takes time to shot these floats correctly.
The best way of doing it is with the aid of a
bucket of water at home, and not on the
river bank. (69)

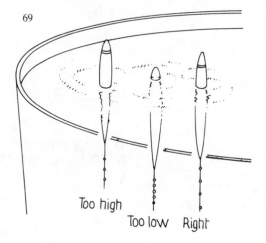

69

Too high
Too low   Right

SWIMFEEDERS

These are plastic cylinders that are weighted,
and either open at both ends or closed (called
block-ends) and can be attached to the line
and used to place groundbait by the hook-bait
where it is needed. There are a number of
models on the market.

- Open-end feeders are secured to the line by
  a loop. They are packed with groundbait
  which is washed free in the current. (70)

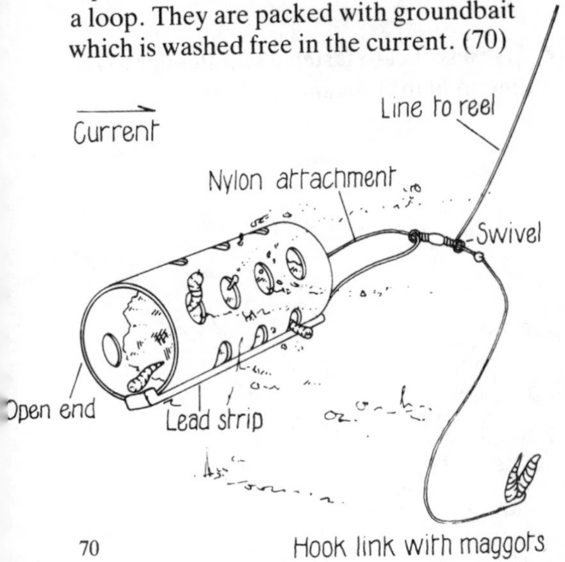

70

Hook link with maggots

■ Block-end feeders can be used to hold
  maggots that wriggle and wash free into the
  swim. (71)

Block-end swimfeeder

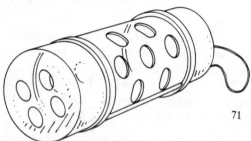

71

■ Use a swivel to fasten a swimfeeder to the
  line; it helps prevent line kink. (72)

72

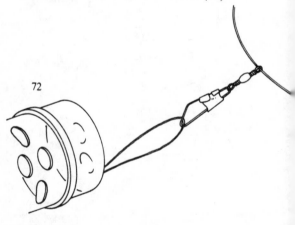

■ The swimfeeder takes the place of the
weight when float-legering, but it is more
usual to use it with the pure leger rig. (73)

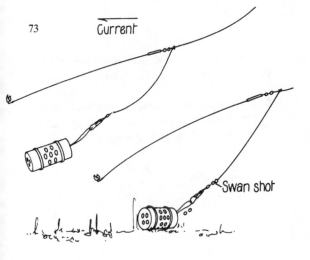

73   Current

Swan shot

PIKE-FISHING RIGS

Whether you are live or deadbaiting, three basic rigs are used in pike fishing.

- Unless you are fishing in very shallow water, the live or suspended deadbait rig is usually supported by a sliding float. (74)

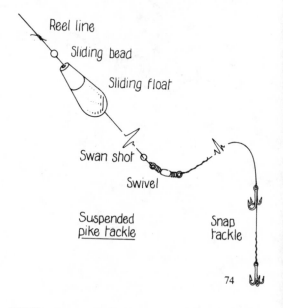

Reel line

Sliding bead

Sliding float

Swan shot

Swivel

Suspended
pike tackle

Snap
tackle

74

■ The paternostered live or deadbait rig is
similar to that used for perch but with
stronger tackle. (75)

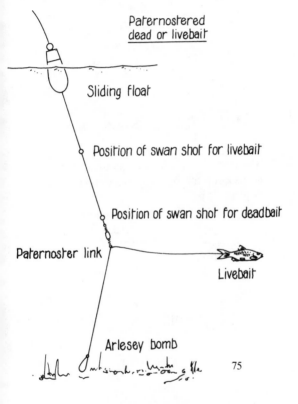

Paternostered
<u>dead or livebait</u>

Sliding float

Position of swan shot for livebait

Position of swan shot for deadbait

Paternoster link

Livebait

Arlesey bomb

75

■ The float-leger is another popular pike rig,
most anglers using the sunken-float method
which keeps the line clear of the bottom

and stops it drifting. A useful rig where there are known to be snags. (76)

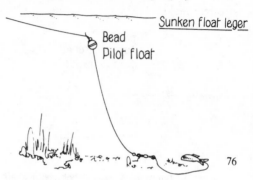

Sunken float leger

Bead
Pilot float

76

■ Some anglers prefer to troll using a float. It helps keep the bait at a pre-determined depth. (77)

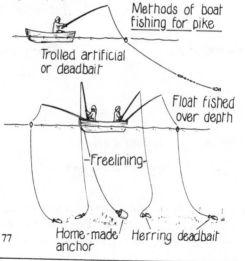

Methods of boat fishing for pike

Trolled artificial or deadbait

Float fished over depth

–Freelining–

77

Home-made anchor

Herring deadbait

LEGER RIGS

More difficult than float-fishing, legering means presenting a bait without the use of a float. Bites are harder to detect and analyse and there is little help from the water to manoeuvre a bait. But with practice it is possible to estimate what a fish is doing to the bait by vibrations transmitted back along the line and rod tip to the angler. It is also possible in running water to work the bait into areas that cannot be reached by casting.

Why and where do you use the leger? When weather conditions are so bad that using a float would be impossible, and where the sheer expanse of water is too big to cast with light tackle. But modern legering is not a matter of using heavy weight and long casts. One can leger on stillwaters and present a bait with great accuracy and delicacy. To do that it is necessary to know about the weights used in legering.

Leger Weights

It is now illegal to use lead in weights smaller than 1oz (see page 43) and anything lighter must be one of the lead substitutes. Some anglers made their own shot but the new legislation largely prevents this.

- As the name suggests, coffin leads are shaped like a coffin with a hole bored through the centre. Being flat they do not move around once they touch bottom, and are used for fast-flowing waters such as weir-pools and places where it is necessary to keep the bait stationary. (78)

78

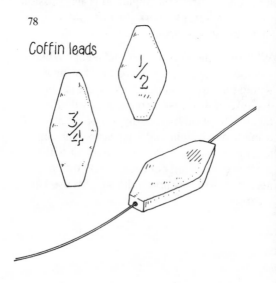

Coffin leads

■ The Arlesey bomb was designed by the late, famous Richard Walker for use in exceptionally deep waters — principally gravel pits. He wanted the lead to sink without twisting the line, and to sink in a straight line. The pear shape and in-built swivel of this leger lead was the perfect answer. (79)

79   Arlesey bombs

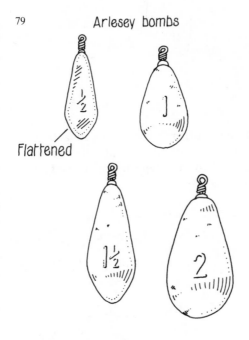

Flattened

■ Barrel leads — sometimes called barleycorns — are long and cylindrical.

Able to roll but not to turn end to end, they are occasionally used as searching leger rigs. (80)

Barrel leads

80

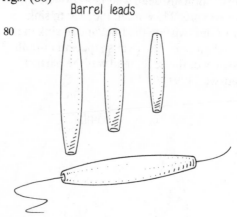

■ Bullet leads are perfectly round, and can roll at will with the current. The angler can use this to advantage in moving the bait around. (81)

Bullet leads

81

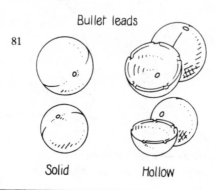

Solid   Hollow

■ Swimfeeders can be purchased with
different shapes and weights in the form of
strip metal fastened along their length. They
not only provide weight for casting, but
groundbait at the same time. (82)

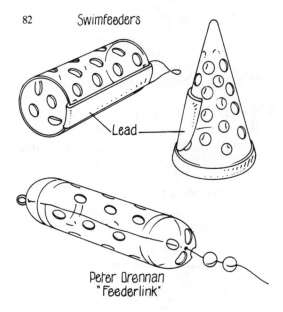

82   Swimfeeders

Lead

Peter Drennan
"Feederlink"

Leger Stops

To stop the weight from sliding down the line
to the hook it is necessary to have a stop. There
are various forms.

■ The matchstick secured by two half-hitches
 is universal when using a bullet lead. It
 allows line to pull free without friction. (83)

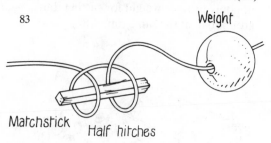

83

Weight

Matchstick   Half hitches

■ The crimped split-shot is often used — but
 this can damage the line if crimped too
 tightly with the pliers, or slide down the line
 if not tight enough. (84)

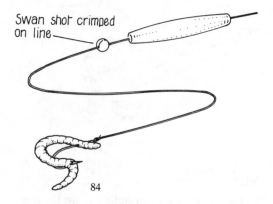

Swan shot crimped
on line

84

■ Swivel stops are popular and work well. But
 they do not stop the weight from putting a

twist in the line. To prevent that it is
necessary to have a second swivel mounted
above the lead itself. (85)

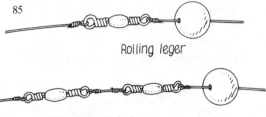

Rolling leger

Two swivels help
avoid line twist

■ Leger stops purchased at the tackle shop
are fool-proof and worth the money. They
are not easy to find if dropped in grass or
mud, so buy several packets at a time. (86)

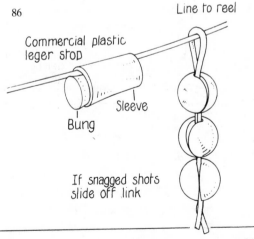

86

Line to reel

Commercial plastic
leger stop

Sleeve

Bung

If snagged shots
slide off link

Static Leger

■ In this style the angler attaches sufficient
lead in the line to hold the bottom, and casts
in front of the swim, keeping the rod in its
rests and a tight line between line and lead.
The smallest attention from a fish will
register by movement of the rod tip. (87)

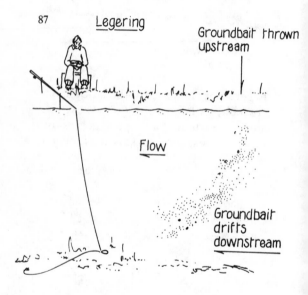

87   Legering

Groundbait thrown
upstream

Flow

Groundbait
drifts
downstream

Rolling Leger

■ A pierced bullet, stopped by a matchstick, allows the current to roll and move both weight and bait. A good tip is to enlarge the hole at the ends of the bullet so that line is not trapped. (88)

88 <u>Rolling leger in running water</u>

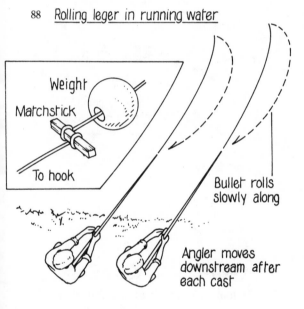

Weight

Matchstick

To hook

Bullet rolls slowly along

Angler moves downstream after each cast

Long-range Leger

■ The streamlined Arlesey bomb together
with the use of a swivel and protective
rubber float-cap make this rig ideal for
really long-distance casting. Use baits that
stay on the hook while casting — lobworms
are ideal. (89)

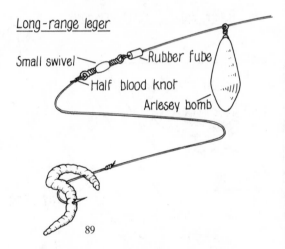

Long-range leger

Small swivel

Rubber tube

Half blood knot

Arlesey bomb

89

Link Leger

■ The feature of this leger is a split ring,
stopped when the cast is made by the hook
eye but which allows the bait to run free
once the rig reaches the bottom. The link
also helps to prevent a fish feeling resistance
when picking up the bait. (90)

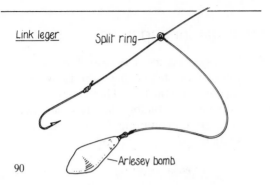

Link leger

Split ring

Arlesey bomb

90

Fixed-link Leger

■ An easy rig to use on a cold day when frozen fingers will not cope with fine tackle. The use of two link swivels means that the hook-link or the leger weight can be changed instantly. (91)

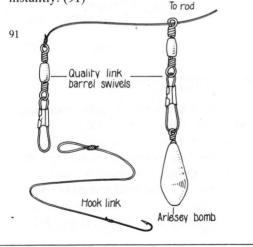

91

To rod

Quality link barrel swivels

Hook link

Arlesey bomb

Swimfeeder Legering

■ This is a deadly method, using the swimfeeder instead of a weight. Leave a long link, with the baited hook and swimfeeder reasonably close to each other so that groundbait brings fish close to the hookbait. (92)

92   Swimfeeder legering

Flow

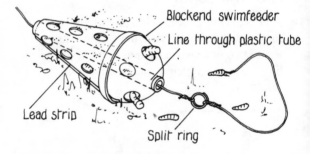

Blockend swimfeeder
Line through plastic tube
Lead strip
Split ring

Paper-bag Legering

■ The use of a paper bag to hold groundbait where the swim is not too distant and can be reached by gentle casting is one method of groundbaiting and weighting at the same time. As the bag falls apart the bait is released — and the hookbait is also allowed to run free. The rig shown is for eels, but it can apply equally to other species. (93)

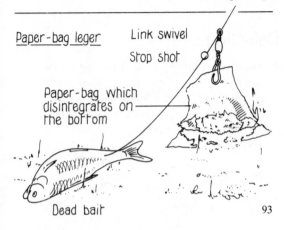

Leger Rigs

Paper-bag leger

Link swivel

Stop shot

Paper-bag which disintegrates on the bottom

Dead bait

93

Swan-shot Legering

■ Swan shot clipped to a link of nylon looped over the reel line makes a delicate rig for any fish. Weight can be added or removed in an instant. (94)

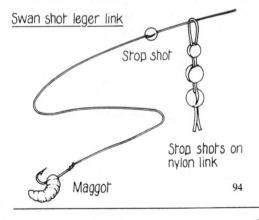

Swan shot leger link

Stop shot

Stop shots on nylon link

Maggot

94

Detecting Bites

- There are many ways of detecting the bite of a taking fish, some simple, some complicated as here. Whichever method you use, for success and a hooked fish every time the secret is practice.
(95)

95

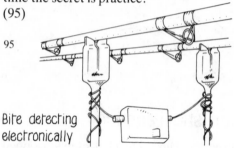

Bite detecting
electronically

Touch Legering

- With this style, the rod is held in the hand and the line between lead and rod kept taut so that the angler can feel taps as a fish

96

attacks the bait. Touch-legering is especially useful when fishing fast waters for barbel. (96)

Rod Rests

■ With the rod supported in rests so that it cannot move, any bite will be recorded at the tip. The angler must be seated so that he can pick the rod up immediately and there should be a high ratio of hooked fish to bites. A piece of folded silver paper pinched on to the line below the rod tip will indicate bites. (97, 98)

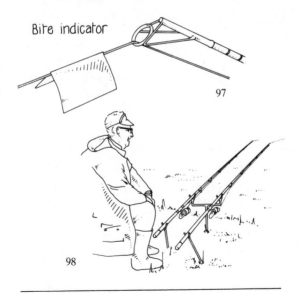

Bite indicator

97

98

Butt Indicators

■ If the rod is held in two rests, the line can be
   looped through a rubber band, or weighted
   by a ball of paste squeezed onto the line
   between reel and first rod ring. In either
   case a taking fish will pull line and either
   slide it from the bands or lift the paste ball.
   (99)

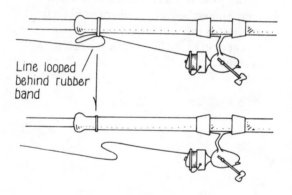

Line looped
behind rubber
band

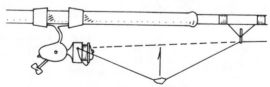

Ball of paste pinched to line which
straightens when fish takes

99

Swingtips

■ Useful on stillwaters, this rod tip extension
is screwed into the end ring of the rod lying
at right-angles to the water. Attention from
a fish will lift it — the movement depending
on the strength of the bite. (100)

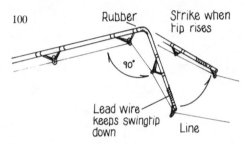

100   Rubber   Strike when
                 tip rises

90°

Lead wire
keeps swingtip
down   Line

Quivertips

■ It is better to use a quivertip where the
current is strong. The stiff, small joint
screws into the end ring of the rod in the
same way as the swingtip but remains
straight. With the rod adjusted in its rests
the sensitive quiver-tip records the tiniest
touch from a fish. (101)

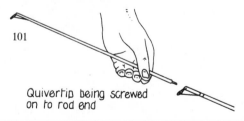

101

Quivertip being screwed
on to rod end

■ An aid many anglers employ to recognise
small bites is the use of a board to isolate
the quivertip from the background of water
or bank. The indicator-board can be plain,
coloured, or marked with a target. (102)

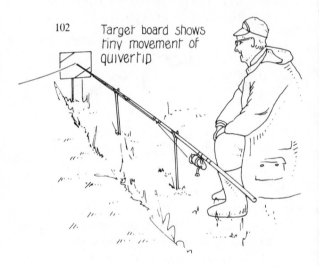

102   Target board shows
tiny movement of
quivertip

INDEX

334